Ninety Years in Montana

Lori Micken

ASPEN SPRINGS PUBLISHING

LIVINGSTON, MONTANA

Ninety Years in Montana

Lori Micken

Copyright © 2023 by Lori Micken.
All rights reserved.

No part of this book may be reproduced, stored
in a retrieval system, or transmitted by any means
without the written permission of the author.

ISBN: 979-8-8547213-4-9

Photo of Lori on back cover by Cheryl Hudson
Cover design and layout by Denis Ouellette

ASPEN SPRINGS PUBLISHING

40 SUNFLOWER LANE
LIVINGSTON, MT 59047

Additional copies available
on Amazon.com

DEDICATION

To my friend of 58 years, Betty Lowery: rancher, college dean, naturalist, scuba diver, fly-fisherwoman, writer, and more, the most capable person I've ever met. She crackled with energy and love of life. She excelled at everything she tried, and she tried about anything. She lived 87 1/2 years before cancer killed her in June. I hope she's at her beloved ranch-her heaven.

ACKNOWLEDGMENTS

My heartfelt thanks to my friends for their help on this book. To Bette Lowery, Carolyn Dickenson, and Carole Evans for encouragement, advice and editing (like, "What in the heck did you mean here?") To Kitty Logan and Lee Micken for scanning photos for the book. I have no computer savy.

INTRODUCTION

My hometown of Cut Bank is on the Montana Hi-Line, the northernmost part of the state along Highway 2 and what used to be the Great Northern Railway right-of-way. As with most of the towns on the Hi-Line, the railroad started it. They constructed a huge iron bridge across Cut Bank Creek Canyon in 1890, ending on the Blackfoot reservation west of the river. Winter camp was made there, and work stopped for the season. The town site was plotted on the east side of the river, off the reservation.

Its winds and brutally cold temperatures are legendary. It is no longer a rowdy oil town, but has settled back into the business of dying. I best know its past.

Come, time travel with me back to a land with no seatbelts, space travel, color photos, ballpoint pens, watermelon in winter, credit cards, kidney and heart transplants, frozen foods, or 1% milk. It was a quiet time with no constant music in stores or when waiting on the phone. Actually, we never had to wait on the phone, as someone either answered or we hung up. We certainly didn't make phone calls anywhere to order things. Yard and hand tools were non-motorized. Stores closed at five, and downtown became deserted except for the bars. Stores did not open on Sundays.

I want my antihistamines, and antibiotics, joint replacements, fast foods, email, movies at home, car-safety devices, washer and dryer, and daily weather reports. So I don't want to go back—only to visit mentally.

Now there is much talk of the values of getting out to Nature. We could hardly get away from Her back then. Flies, mosquitoes, and various garden pests; colder, snowier winters; unpredicted thunderstorms and high winds; the northern lights; glorious, soft spring and summer days; stars undimmed by electric lights of the neighboring town; vast miles without houses in the country; and plenty of empty lots in town to explore. Nature surrounded us.

People say they need to "find themselves." I never had to find me; I was right there, close and comfortable all the time.

Part 1
Cut Bank

POETRY

At about 12 years old, I started carrying a pencil and small spiral notebook so I could write down my thoughts. I was still wearing bib overalls like Grandpa's, so there was a pocket in front for the notebook and another for the pencil. All I have left of those writings are these two poems that Mom had saved in a scrapbook. Mostly I wrote about moths, bees, and other bugs I'd found. Later, I wrote about our horseback-riding adventures.

SUNSET

Delicate lace, edging to pink sewn on a dress of blue,

Some people picture a sunset sky in colors of baby hue.

Montana's skies, different than those, blaze with a prism's light.

Scarlett and orange and sapphire blue deepen to purple velvet night.

I remember looking out the bathroom window into the back yard when I wrote this one. It's not great poetry, a step or two above doggerel, but I am amazed at my preteen self writing these.

A need to write is a powerful urge, one that is a hard taskmaster. I put myself to sleep at night imagining characters and places or going over a troublesome sentence that I had written that day. Often, I find in the morning those mazingly wonderful lines I jotted at bedtime are not at all usable, in fact barely intelligible. But the joy of writing keeps me going anyway.

COUNTRY SCENE

Once I looked out upon the night.
Mother Earth slumbered under a robe of ermine,
Her hair of soft gray drifted,
Waving under a crown of diamonds
Surmounted by a huge, opaque pearl
That lit the millions of tiny sequins in her ermine wrap
And showed the tails of fence posts
Even more black against the white robe:
Winter had come.

CHICKENS

World War Two colored every facet of our lives, as movies, and newspapers predominantly covered the war. We on the "home front" expected to do without, and rationing made certain that we did. I don't recall ever really going without anything except candy.

As one patriotic duty, the government encouraged growing Victory Gardens. Motivated by this propaganda, I wanted one. My ever-indulgent grandfather okayed the project. Our backyard had maybe two inches of soil over solid sandstone. Grandpa made a frame of two by eights about 12 feet long and four feet wide at the back of the house. He had topsoil brought in to fill it. My patriotism could go forth.

I planted radishes, Swiss chard, peas, and carrots. Grandma added a row of tansy at the far end, outside the box, as a bug deterrent. She also planted a patch of chives for her soups and stews. The garden prospered, and we had fresh veggies to help achieve victory.

On many of the propaganda posters, Uncle Sam also encouraged backyard chicken flocks. I didn't think about what city people could do to be patriotic. Maybe they built the ships and tanks and planes. At any rate the second winter of the war, I set up a campaign to get chickens. In

June Grandpa ordered a brooder and chicks from the Great Falls Purina store.

A white garage set on the back of our lot, along with an unpainted shed housing an outhouse and an equal sized empty room. Most winters we actually still used the outhouse as the water and/or sewer pipes would often freeze. Grandpa gave me the spare room for a chicken coop. Fortunately it had an electric plug-in.

After an agonizing wait, the brooder arrived. Half of it had a solid metal covering, the other half wire. It had a thermometer, feed trays, and a water dish. Grandpa insisted I read the manual and follow the instructions, setting up the correct temperature long before the chicks came.

Finally, the day arrived for the 25 chicks to come in on the first passenger train of the day. Grandma and I went to the post office to get them. Several other people had orders coming, too, and the peeping could be heard on opening the post office door.

I picked up my small cardboard box with many holes in it. Peeking into one, I saw a mass of pale-yellow down, sharp beaks, and bright black eyes. My babies, my very own patriotic chicks flock! Grandma and I walked through the alley, a block away, through the back gate and deposited the box in the chicken coop—no longer just a shed. I started removing them one by one, but she insisted I hurry lest they get cold, so I scooped them out by the double handful. They all looked healthy and almost immediately started eating and drinking. This was a great relief to me, as I had feared I would have to teach them.

Grandma went back to the house, but I spent a rapt hour watching my new babies. Grandpa looked in on them when he came home for lunch and reminded me to check on them every three hours: the temperature, and their water and food. As an afterthought he said, "You'll need the alarm clock to get up during the night. And use the flashlight outside."

Night. I hadn't thought of that. I was afraid of the dark. Hopefully no one knew. My cousins and I walked home from movies in the dark, but there were big lights on both corners high on the power poles, and there were four of us. I would occasionally venture into the front yard after dark, but the porch light and streetlight protected me. Darkness could hide most anything.

After lunch I got out a tablet and pencil. If I stayed up to 10 o'clock, it still would be light outside. I would have to go out in the dark at 1 o'clock and 4 o'clock. By 7 o'clock, it would be daylight. Twice for a whole week, 14 times into that black backyard. Crooks, the mummy, the Frankenstein monster all came out at night. Probably lots of other stuff I didn't know about: Owls, bats, werewolves, unnamed demons.

I knew the chicks would die if I didn't take proper care of them. If I confessed I was too frightened to go out, Gramps would give them to Uncle Bob.

The alarm went off at 1 o'clock, I shut it off and took the flashlight from under my bed and got up. Gram warned me not to turn on bedroom or living room lights thus awakening them. I made it through the living room and kitchen into the bathroom, shut the door, and turned on the light. I had left my shoes and jacket there. I put them on and rolled up the shade so light could be a beacon. I also opened the window so my death screams could be heard in the house. I left the light on, went back out through the kitchen, the shed, and outside. The flashlight beam seemed only a pitiful glow as I went down the steps, across the uneven stone patio, and into the yard. As I swept the flashlight beam around, shadows moved. The trees and lilac bush Gram had planted were too small for anything to hide behind. Nobody hung from the clothesline. I reached the coop, breathing hard with a tom-tom heartbeat. No other sounds touched my ears.

I opened the coop door. Vague peeps made me smile. Temperature, food, and water were okay. The 25 babies huddled together, asleep under the heater.

I stepped back outside and looked over the yard. The bathroom window light was reassuring. Then I looked up. The sky made me gasp. I've seen stars at night of course, but these were extra bright, extra beautiful. I forgot about all the bogymen and walked to mid-yard, gazing all around the sky. The short walk to the house was no longer fearsome. The 4 o'clock alarm wakened me, and I repeated the trip without the bathroom window light. I even turned off the flashlight to stand in the dark. I had beaten my fear by finding beauty in what I feared. At 10 3/4 years old I had learned a valuable life lesson, realizing how ridiculous I had been. Weight seemed to lift off me. I could be brave and face alone whatever fear threatened me all the rest of my life.

GAMES AND PLAY

When I was young, we thought the game of musical chairs was hilarious fun. To play, a circle of chairs was made with one seat less than the number playing. Someone at the piano played a few bars of music while we marched around the circle, aware that when the music stopped, one person would not be able to find a seat. He or she was eliminated in the play. This was repeated until there was only one, the winner, left.

"Let's play, `Heavy, heavy, hangs over your head,'" someone might suggest. "That's fun. We can sit still awhile. I'm tired of this one," someone else would say, and we would organize for the new game.

This required the same circle of chairs with everyone seated, facing center. The hostess often officiated so everyone could play. She moved around the circle collecting some personal item from each: a hair barrette, a handkerchief, a belt, a pocketknife, etc. The hostess then stood behind the chair of one player, selected an item from her assortment and intoned the words, "Heavy, heavy, hangs over your head. What shall the owner do to redeem it?"

Because this player did not know what was being held over his or her head, he or she tried to think of something unusual, something ridiculous or embarrassing. The one selected might say, "Dance a jig." "Recite a poem." "Untie Mary's shoe laces," or the ultimate in daring, "Kiss your best girl."

The latter brought screams of laughter. The owner of the item responded usually with reluctance or outright refusal, but he or she would be urged, teased, cajoled, even pushed forward until some kind of response was forthcoming.

A variation of this game was called spin the bottle. When a milk or pop bottle was spun in the middle of the circle, it came to rest pointing at the player who had to respond to the orders of the spinner. He then had his turn to spin and give orders.

Oddly enough, I learned about the game "gossip" in Sunday school. The first person in line whispers a phrase into the next person's ear, and this is repeated to the next person until the last person tells what she or he heard. Even with young ears and good hearing, the phrase is generally mangled.

Of course, we played hide and seek, jacks, marbles, tag, pom-pom-pull-away, and others I've forgotten. My three cousins and I would often make up games, two against two. One late afternoon, we took a yardstick and threw it up over the power line running into the house. One of the other team would throw it back after catching it midair. If it hit the wire or the ground, it didn't count. We scored the game a point per catch. Game ended with darkness and being called home.

Throwing a ball over the porch roof to hit on the attic wall was another game we invented. We'd scramble to catch the return bounce, the ball catcher getting to throw it. Grandma usually ended the sport, yelling at us to stop, that we'd ruined her nap, or the noise bothered her reading.

We would also punch two holes in the top sides of tin cans, put strings through the holes, tie them to our feet, and walk around in these mini-stilts. A lot of pushing and shoving occurred to try to knock each other off balance.

No adults supervised us, taught the correct way to throw a ball, or gave us rules for a game. There were no organized sports, such as baseball or basketball for gradeschoolers. At recess the class leaders organized the games, not the teachers. Or we played on the slide, monkey rings, or swings. We stood on the swing seat, holding onto the chain supports, and pumped ourselves higher and higher until the chain went slack, giving a thrilling sag and jolt. Braver (or dumber) souls would jump off the swing just as the seat started an upward arc. If seated, this wasn't too bad, but often led to a poor landing if done from the standing position.

Such a fun world we lived in. Time was endless. Joy came every day. Scrapes and slivers were quickly forgotten, as was anger at each other. We were independent, inventive, and free in a play world all our own.

HIGH SCHOOL GATHERINGS

Most high school memories have faded, but there are little snippets that stand out.

Our class of 1950 counted only 39 students out of a total high-school enrollment of 168. We and the junior class of 43 people were the last of the depression kids. The town's population jumped from 845 in 1930 to 2509 in 1940, a 196% increase. And it kept growing. Oil and gas exploration pushed the growth.

We endured freshman initiation. Mostly, our faces were painted with lipstick; we were ridiculed as dumb freshmen and made to carry upperclassman's books for them. Some of the guys were taken out in the country and forced to run barefoot through stubble fields with their tormentors following in a car to light their way and make sure they ran. I'm still horrified at the memory, but I don't recall who any of the fellows were. I can't imagine the damage done to their feet, or why perpetrators weren't caught.

Miss Stufft taught Home Economics. We figured she was rich because she wore a fur coat in the nastiest weather, along with big, baggy snow pants, popular then, and heavy winter boots. By class time, she had changed to her usual elegant clothing.

We girls took Home Ec. The guys took shop classes. I remember cooking and sewing classes and some exercises on table manners and how to walk properly. Ann Jones, my riding buddy, and I partnered in the kitchen. We tinkered with recipes and illegally put twice the vanilla in any recipe calling for it. Alice Essex, in the kitchen next to us, frowned on our mischief but never tattled.

My grandmother had taught me to run a sewing machine, so I had no difficulty with our first freshman assignment of hemming a dishtowel. For the advanced project, I made a shirt of blue chambray. I embroidered raccoon heads on the two pockets and a horse head on back. My sophomore sewing project became a disaster. I chose white nylon for a very puffy-sleeved blouse with long button cuffs. I wore it once and washed it. It partially disintegrated.

Ann and I dabbled in cooking at home, too. During the war, rationed goods included sugar. Stores seldom had any candy, including marshmallows. Grandma had somehow laid hands on a 100-pound sack of sugar before rationing started, so we tried making marshmallows at my house. Looking back, I suppose we didn't get a high enough temperature when cooking, and the marshmallows didn't solidify. We put in more sugar, recooked, poured, and still it remained semi-liquid, so we repeated. Gram wakened from her afternoon nap and interfered that third time around. It never did harden to anything but spoon texture but tasted like marshmallows. Grandma reprimanded us for the waste of sugar but didn't really get mad.

Another time Grandma had bought Concord grapes to make jelly. The next day friends invited her to ride with them to the Flathead to visit Uncle Bob. She told me to make the jelly. I'd helped her many times so felt fairly confident. Of course, I asked Ann to help. We soon ran into problems and phoned Miss Stufft for help—several times. The jelly turned out fine. I hope I gave Miss Stufft some.

Ann once helped me make a turkey dinner for my family. We decided to baste the turkey with wine, as we had read somewhere that this would enhance the flavor. We also sampled the wine at each basting. As usual, Grandma napped, so we had no supervision. We were pretty giggly by the time it was cooked, but it was a superb roast turkey.

In one freshman cooking class, a messenger came to escort me to the principal's office. I couldn't imagine what I had done wrong and was very frightened. Two men stood in the outer office with Mr. Haburchack, the principal. The taller of the two asked, "Do you know who I am?"

"Yes," I said. "You are Gehres Weed, my father." I had seen a picture of him, a newspaper clipping, but had never met him. Beyond that I have no memory, but we chatted a few minutes. He and his brother, George, had come to town on business, and he decided to meet me.

I can't recall my emotions other than thinking I looked horrible with flour on my apron and hands, and probably my usual disheveled hair. I know Uncle Bob and Aunt Joe kept him informed of my progress through the years, and sent pictures, so he probably wasn't too taken aback. I must've been in a state of shock to not remember anything else about so momentous an event.

The school required four years of English. Miss Betty Madison, a first year teacher, taught the senior literature class. She was a very pretty young woman, and the guys were enchanted with her. She wore heavy horn rim glasses, probably to make herself look older, or perhaps a bit menacing.

Between classes one of the guys took the grill off a heat vent in her room, put some Limburger cheese in the opening, and replaced the grill. When it started heating up, Miss Madison went over, closed the room door, and continued to teach. The perpetrator raised his hand and asked permission to clean out the stench. She never blinked an eye, or broke a smile.

Shortly before Christmas vacation "Breeze" Harris raised his hand, stood and asked her to the senior ball with him. He was two years older than the rest of us, and so probably only two years her junior. She thanked him and said, "I'm sorry, Breeze, but I already have a date." Bill Pyper turned out to be her future husband. It all ended well for Breeze many years later. After her husband died, he asked Betty to marry him, and she did.

The school required two years of math: algebra as freshmen and geometry as sophomores. The former mystified some of us gals. We tried studying it together, but none of us could grasp the concepts very well. I did end up with a "C." Geometry was another matter. I loved it and hoped to take solid geometry, but it was offered only on alternate years and I couldn't fit it into my schedule, probably for the best. Calculus was available too, but it smelled too much of algebra.

Our school was well endowed because of the oil fields swelling the tax base. Other schools came to see and emulate our model Home Ec department.

Mac Johnson taught an aeronautics class. The course included use of a link trainer in the basement. I snuck down to look at the machine. I desperately wanted to take the class, but when I found the amount of math involved, desperation faded.

Joe Strizich taught biology, my favorite subject of all four years. I thought he looked like a Nazi SS man: big, husky, rough-featured, with a crew cut. I was a rapt student.

The first semester, he assigned us to keep a notebook of newspaper and magazine articles, pictures, whatever we could find about biology. About a week before the deadline,

I realized I had done nothing toward the scrapbook. I scrambled and scrounged, even cutting a page out of a biology book in a science set I had. I received a C- on the slipshod work. I'm not sure I deserved that much.

One day after school, Ann and I went into the biology lab to look at the preserved specimens that we never had time to see during class. We even found a couple of things my uncles had contributed to the collection 22 years before. We spent more time than we had intended, and when we started to leave, we found ourselves locked in the room. Fortunately, the windows opened, so we started yelling and finally drew the attention of someone passing by on the sidewalk. He came in the building and got us released.

We had the choice of Latin or Spanish as a foreign language. I opted for Latin, as my grandparents said it would be good for me. We had a new teacher, Mr. Swanberg. He told all his student to call him Swanny. He taught Latin as though it were a living language, an innovation far ahead of his time. After the first couple weeks, we were to speak only Latin in class. We had to make our own little Latin dictionaries of new words with pictures to define them. We sang Christmas carols he had translated into Latin and didn't touch the usual mechanics of the language. Unfortunately, he was not hired back. The next year. Clarence Spetch taught the old-fashioned way. I never quite caught on to declensions and other fine points on language structure, so Latin II was nine months of misery and average grades.

Apparently, my grades in other subjects were slumping, too, so Grandpa sank to bribing me. He would give me a dollar for each "A," 50 cents for a "B," and a dollar returned to him if I fell to a "C." After a couple six weeks' report cards garnering me very little money, I decided to, as Grandpa would say, "cut my head in" and bring up grades.

Nickolas Haburchack, (some of the guys called him Nickel-Ass Hab-a-crappy), our principal, taught chemistry. He had to leave class quite often, being called out to the office. This left a bunch of juniors and seniors more or less on our own to complete the lab or read the next assignment.

Of course, Ann and I were lab partners, along with Joyce Varis. For some reason, we three decided to use sulfuric acid to burn a hole through the drawer bottom in our lab table. It took many trips of sneaking into the storage room for a few drops of the acid, but eventually we succeeded. I shudder at the memory.

We had learned to make hydrogen sulfide in one chem lab. In the teacher's absence, we set up a generator, attached it to a long piece of rubber tubing, and inserted the other end in the keyhole to the biology lab, which was next door. Joyce, Ann, and I had the apparatus ready to dismantle each time we heard Mr. Strizich's first steps toward the door to find the source of the rotten egg smell. Joyce rolled the tubing, Ann removed the stopper and replaced it with a solid one, and I did the disconnections. We put it all in a drawer. He never caught us, possibly because we were looked on as some of the good kids and above suspicion.

Coach Willie DeGroot taught American history. In the spring he opened the room windows in nice weather. One of the guys chewed tobacco. When DeGroot turned to write on the board, the student would stand and spit out the window. He timed it wrong once and coach saw him, walked over, shut the window, and continued talking while he stood there. People really can turn green. Forced to swallow the cud, the lad raced from the room. History lecture kept on without a break.

In our senior year, most of the guys dated underclass girls, leaving us gals to date underclass boys. Ann dated a junior, Monte Fauque, her future husband. I dated Wayne Coursey, a sophomore in band with me. Monte has his own car. One late evening, we four decided to go to Shelby, 25 miles east, and change their big "S" on the hill coming into town to a "C." We scrambled up to it from the road and rolled the white rocks in the lower part of the S down the hill. The next week, as retribution, some of the Shelby students painted our gym steps maroon and gold, their school colors. No one, either school, ever stepped forward to confess.

Later that year, one of our classmates came to Ann and me in tears to confess she had an F in English. If she did flunk, she would not graduate. So we tutored her during study hall and she passed: my first teaching success.

The last week of high school arrived. Senior Sneak Day took us on a bus trip west on Highway 2 to Lake Blaine. The highlight of the day, however, came as we gathered at the school at six that morning. A huge metal sign of a colorful smiling cavalier had been hung from the roof of the second story of the school. It was an ad for Cavalier Old Style Lager Beer. Six of the guys had driven nearly to Shelby, and chopped and sawed the sign's support posts. They loaded it in their pickup and drove to the back of the school by the shop, where they horsed it up on the roof. It was secured with some wire clothesline they had confiscated.

Oddly enough, neither the school nor law enforcement authorities found out who had done this wonderful prank. It still stands as the best in the school's history. Suspicions pointed to several who might have been guilty, but there was no proof. Just this year I talked to Ed Mitch, one of the young men involved, and found these details. The anonymity of the other five pranksters remains, at the request of Ed.

Graduation came. In the prior years, I'd wondered what it would be like, marching into the gym in cap and gown, not playing in the band, and no longer being a part of that big, noisy family of teenagers. We seniors joined the band to play one piece, and the senior choir members sang one more song with the choir.

Then we were gone.

Lori in band uniform in eighth grade

CUT BANK HIGH SCHOOL BAND

The third floor of Cut Bank High School held only the band. It looks like an afterthought, tacked on up there like a cellblock. Windows looked north toward checkerboard wheat fields that stretched on to Canada. We in the percussion section stood in front of the windows, so we could turn to see more of the view than most. Band met before school around 7:30 AM three days a week. In our senior year, there were 48 band members. The junior high students were part of the group. Almost all of us had started out when in junior high, which is housed in the east wing of the same brick building.

Alice Essex played the glockenspiel—bells for short—a heavy, harp-shaped affair with bars of metal that she struck with a round wooden mallet. She could even handle two at once. In the band room she had a stand for it. When we marched she had a leather harness with a cup like flag-bearers use. She was one tough kid.

Alice often stopped at my house to warm herself briefly in the winter. She had already walked four blocks. One brutally cold morning, possibly the only windless and snow-free one, remains clear in my memory. It was probably 20 below zero or colder. I had never seen the stars so close, so many, so brilliant as that morning. No moon dimmed any of them. Alice and I walked in the middle of the street the three blocks from my door to the high school door. No car came by. The only sounds were our voices, crunching feet, and an imagined sputtering of starlight.

Carol Ann Quigley and Bob Hall played snare drums with me. Bob switched to bass drum for a while but in his senior year decided to be a cheerleader. This was very unique in 1949 and '50. Pat Cunningham and a new girl, Connie Larson, were the other two cheerleaders. Back then students didn't just watch the cheerleaders. We knew all the yells we had learned in pep club meetings and shook the football field bleachers or the rafters of the gymnasium with our cheering.

The only other senior in the band was John Fry, who played the tuba. My best buddy, Ann Jones, had to drop out in her senior year because of a badly broken ankle acquired in a horse race.

Our band uniforms were splendid: purple pants with gold stripe, purple jackets with gold braid, and military style hats—purple and gold, of course, our school colors. We wore white shirts with black ties under the jackets. Unfortunately, the snazzy uniforms were junked spring of our senior year and replaced with loose-fitting tan suits, belted and tied at the waist, no hats. We looked like a bunch of ragged business people. The band played at all home football and basketball games, plus going to Shelby and Browning, the two closest towns. At one football game, again a very cold night, our drumheads all split at the first stroke of the opening roll. We improvised by striking the wood drum edges with the sticks, not much of a rat-a-tat-tat, but okay to march out on the field.

We played for open house, the spring music concert, and the Memorial and Labor Day parades the town put on. In May we traveled to state band festivals, usually in Havre, but one year in Fort Benton. For a small town, we were darned good, usually getting an "A" rating in the competitions. Besides marching the streets of Havre, there were concerts in their auditorium. Two other bands in the festivals stand out in my memory. The Glasgow Scotties had kilt uniforms, and their band director's Scottish terrier mascot marched with them. Canada sent down, probably from Lethbridge, a small pipe-and-drum band. The bass drummer wore a leopard skin across his shoulders and back. He used two sticks, one on each side of the big drum. The three Highland drums sounded deeper and louder than ours. I don't remember how many pipers they had, no more than three or four. It was a very compact, loud group. The hard military beat, the kilts, the pipes all captivated me.

We three snare drummers developed some complicated marching routines, using the rims as well as the heads of our drums. I've no idea who dreamed up the routines, Bob I think, or what signal we used to change from one to another. We were good though! All that marching, stair climbing, and carrying drums and other instruments had to have had us in as good shape as the athletes.

I still appreciate seeing a good marching band, and hearing what we considered the core of it, the booms and rat-a-tat-tats and bells of the percussion section. The praises of our parents and town people made all the time and effort well worthwhile.

SMALL TOWN ENTERTAINMENT AND WORK

Cut Bank, Montana, had less than 1,000 people most of the time before Word War II.

Our one movie theater was called The Orpheum, an ancient, sandstone building, fronted on Central Avenue. Unfortunately, mice infested the place, making a good living on the spilled popcorn and sodas. Movies weren't rated then, so we could go to any of them. Friday and Saturday nights were our only opportunities, as bedtime on school nights was strictly enforced. In summer, we needed no movie entertainment in the long-light days of play.

The schools provided much of the town's entertainment. Every Christmas, the grade school put on a huge show. In first grade, we girls were bells, I don't recall the boys' role. Mothers made the costumes. Ours had a wire loop suspended on some kind of filmy material with a "rope" cord around the waist and hem, rather like tinsel garlands we put on Christmas trees. The tops were plain, sleeveless, of the same flimsy material. We sang some sort of bell song in rhythm with our swinging skirts.

The next-door-neighbor girl, a sixth grader, Sally Lewis, had the enviable part of being the star actress. She played sort of a princess or Faerie Queen. She introduced each act and had a lot of speaking parts. My main ambition then was to get the lead part when I, too, became a sixth grader. It didn't happen, and I always remained some sort of Christmas ornament or icon in the choir.

Other times of the year, classes put on short plays in the basement of the grade school in a small room with a stage. A wonderful, secret trap door on one side of the stage made things magically appear and disappear. Grandma always came to every such state occasion as this, as did many of the mothers.

Mrs. Ellis gave piano lessons in her home. Each spring she put on a piano recital. Or I should say, we students suffered in a piano recital. Each of us had a memorized piece. My last one was "In the Hall of the Mountain King." Lots of thunderous passages and fun to play, but I lived in terror of getting in the middle of a piece and forgetting the ending. Betty Jo Hupp and I played in a duet one year, blessedly with the music in front of us. I know we didn't practice enough times, but as I recall, we got through it very well. This really wasn't a community event, as I can't imagine anyone but parents wanting to suffer through it.

To liven up walks to town, school, or anywhere, my friends and I would pick out a rock and kick it along in front of us, a contest in seeing who could keep it on the sidewalks the longest. This was later on, after sidewalks were put in, of course.

One wonderful summer day my cousins and I found a red-and-black ant colony making war on a black ant colony. The invaders killed most of the black ants and carried off the eggs and larva to their own big nest, a pile of tiny sticks and pieces of grass nearby. Uncle Bob told us the black ants "children" would be used as slaves in the victor's colony. Early humans must have learned from the ants.

I was in seventh grade when Carol Quigley, Bob Hall, and I joined the band to play snare drums. We played together for the next six years. Ours was primarily a marching band and provided the music in the town parades on Memorial Day and one or two other holidays. In the fall and spring in nice weather, we would practice out on the streets of town. People always came out to listen and wave. We marched at halftime in every football game, regardless of the weather. We also played for the basketball games and put on a spring concert with the choir.

Besides high school football, basketball, and track, the school also entertained the town with two plays, one by the juniors and the other by the seniors. I worked as the stage manager on these two events. My good friend Alice Essex had a starring role opposite Bob Hall in the junior play. They revolted over the kissing scene, as neither wanted to perform the act, but the show went on, and I think the actors followed the script.

Cut Bank was a drinking town with a surplus of bars, plus the Elks, Moose, and VFW clubs. The Elks ran a regular gambling casino in the basement and held several "Lost Wages Nights" a year. Eventually this phased out. Our family still owns one of their slot machines.

Dancing and card playing were also major forms of entertainment. We kids played Monopoly, Chinese Checkers, Dominoes and Checkers, plus Go Fish and other card games. Early on Grandpa taught me two types of solitaire, which he played every night.

When the fire siren went off, people who had cars and weren't at work, sometimes those at work, too, raced to follow the fire engines and get in on that excitement. One hideous accident occurred just west of town. An oil tank truck went off the highway high above the river, crashed and burned on the river flat. We never had a car, so my family and I missed out on most of those community events.

Occasionally ice would dam the river and cause flooding. Somehow, everyone knew when the authorities were going to dynamite the ice jam. I did get to see it once when some kind soul offered Gram, Gramps, and me a ride.

Mostly, work filled the time. There were no TV dinners or fast food places, so meals were home cooked. Rarely did we go to a restaurant for dinner. Washing, ironing, mending, and cleaning were all labor-intensive, with automatic washers and dryers unheard of. Clothes and linens were mended; shirt collars turned front to back to lengthen wear. Hand-me-downs and kids' clothes made from lightly worn parts of adult clothes or flour sacks were common.

Grandma didn't own a vacuum cleaner, although I suppose some people had them. She cleaned the living room carpet with a hand-pushed sweeper and took the rug out to the clothesline every spring to beat the dust out. Curtains had to be taken down to wash every spring, and the house cleaned once a week, maybe. The cleanliness level stood far below our standards now.

For a long time, the residential streets remained unpaved, so there was a lot of dust. It could be driven by the nearly constant wind.

Grandpa took down the window screens every fall and put up storm windows in their place. In the spring, he reversed the process.

Most houses didn't have attic insulation, revealed in winter by the snow melting off the roofs on all but the eaves. I don't know if our house had insulation in the walls. There were certainly no R-factors to be considered, as materials like sawdust or ash from the trains' boilers were used for insulation. Fortunately, cheap natural gas came from the oil and gas fields up north. One stove in the corner of the living room by the bedroom door provided most of our heat. Grandma's cook stove in the kitchen helped warm the place with her baking and boiling great kettles of soup or stew or scrapple. Grandpa hung his heavy jacket over the doorknob in winter to cut some of the draft coming in.

Don't get me wrong, it was a good life. We had plenty of time to read, to watch insects, to visit face-to-face with friends and family, and to play. Entertainment often came from within oneself, a fine place. I think it would do everyone in this electronic age some good to go back 75 years and live for a day, to slow the pace, to enjoy the community, and be more self-reliant for entertainment.

RAINBOW GIRLS

Eastern Star is a branch of the Masons for women; DeMolay Boys, a branch for teenage boys; and Rainbow Girls for teenage girls. They are all secret societies. As my family was Masonic, as soon as I turned 13 I applied to join Rainbow Girls and was accepted. The next year, I held the office of outer observer, a good place for an ill-poised, socially-unacceptable freshman. I sat outside the closed meeting door and admitted any late arrivals with the proper knocks and announcement.

That fall I had gone out horseback riding on Monday and stayed a bit too late. I raced home to change to a formal but did not take time for a bath, nylons, or good shoes. It was easier to run the four blocks to the Masonic Temple in my moccasins, anyway. I just made it in time to join in the officers' entry march for the meeting. The knock—knock of formally closing the door to the meeting accomplished, I sprawled comfortably in my chair: feet out and well apart, back slumped, set to relive the day's ride.

Holy cats! Here came the Order of Eastern Star's Worthy Matron, sweeping up the hall under full sail, her beautiful formal swishing, gold chain and flower in the braids on top of her head, the jewels of her office swinging on her breasts. Unfortunately, that same prestigious person was my Aunt Joe. Her family had moved to the Flathead the year before, in 1946, and she had decided to continue to move up through the chairs to the head of the chapter. She commuted by train to meetings and other required social events, such as attending our Rainbow Girls meeting. The train from the west had been a little late that evening. She took an eternity to upbraid me for my footgear, horse smell, posture, and general disheveled look.

"Yes, I had combed my hair, I think. Yes, I've been riding. Yes, a young lady should not sit like that. No, it would never happen again. Yes, I was sorry to have desecrated my office and all of Rainbow Girls here in the present, and in the past and future."

Somehow, I remembered the correct knocks, opened the door and announced to the inner observer that the head of Eastern Star wished to attend the meeting. After she was admitted, the door closed, I made the appropriate answering knocks, still stinging from the castigation. I sat with feet together and posture erect, lest another Goddess of Wrath descend on me.

My next office in Rainbow was organist. Again, out of sight, but in the choir loft above the assembly. My skills as a pianist were barely sufficient to play the easy marches for the assembly.

One horrible night I somehow knocked the music book off the piano just as the major event of voting on potential members came up. The only piece in my tiny repertoire of memorized music I could recall was the western "Streets of Laredo," about the dying cowboy, certainly a solemn piece. I cut the tempo and added a couple of what I hoped were stately chords, and played. Our Mother Advisor, Mrs. Wilkins, and some of the girls looked up at me with raised eyebrows at hearing a tune other than the prescribed one. On the next break, I retrieved my music and finished the meeting correctly.

At Easter the DeMolay Boys and Rainbow Girls would meet at the Masonic Temple, pair up and walk to the Presbyterian Church three blocks away to attend church service together. We wore formals, the guys in suits, wearing capes over them.

Each summer our chapter went to the cemetery for a day to fix up the old, uncared-for graves. Everyone met at the Masonic Temple and drove out to Crown Hill Cemetery two miles north of town. For two years, I rode my horse to the workdays, timing it to get there with the others. We returned to town for root beer floats and snacks. At least for this event, I was appropriately dressed.

To raise money one year, we sold the sheet music for our state song. Alice Essex and I were not very good door-to-door sales persons, but Alice hit on the idea of going to skid row—the block of Central Avenue with all the bars. The fuzzy-brained men on the street happily helped us out, giving money but not wanting the sheet music. One guy even gave us five dollars! We raked in a lot of money and still had most of the music to sell legitimately.

When a senior I finally made the meeting room as one of the seven colors of the Rainbow officers. I marched in, proper shoes, no horse aroma, poised and confident. Too bad Aunt Joe no longer served as Worthy Matron of Eastern Star. She had tried valiantly, sporadically, and fruitlessly to make a lady of me. This was and is as close as I came.

The highest honor in rainbow girls is being awarded the Grand Cross of Colors. I think I received it for longevity and good attendance, certainly not for high office or exemplary achievements.

I attended the state Rainbow Girls' meeting in Livingston the year I graduated, 1950. Three others of the chapter and our Mother Advisor made the long drive.

That was the last of being a Rainbow Girl.

EACH STAR'S A POOL OF WATER

Ann Jones and I were best pals from babyhood through school. We lived two blocks apart. I would cross the street and an empty lot, go down the alley, across Second Avenue, through her alley, and in the back door for visits. In the summer, we would set up a Monopoly game in their basement rec room on the last day of school and continue the same game until Labor Day. If I remember correctly, I was always bankrupt and broke long before September, but we still kept playing every rainy day.

Mostly, we rode horseback together. We'd bicycle out east of town a mile to Humble's ranch where we pastured our horses. Sometimes we'd ride through town to go west into the Cut Bank River Canyon and explore upstream or downstream. The river is the boundary between the Blackfoot reservation and Glacier County proper. We might ford the river and go out on the reservation to the airport, to Indian Springs (with ice-cold alkali drinking water), or to the waterfall.

Several small streams snake their way across the prairies. One poured about ten feet over a sandstone slab into a sizable pool. It was a great place for a picnic with lots of bushes growing along the pool and up the banks by the waterfall, as well as in the 150-foot depression beyond. We could access the same area by heading south two miles from Humble's pasture, fording the river, and continuing out on the reservation. There were very few fences then and we only had to open and close two gates to get to the river. Then it was all open country for many miles.

There were a few dirt roads out in the area that led to oil-company pump houses for completed oil wells. Long metal rods that slid back and forth on cupped stands led from the pump house to the wells. Some of these extended a considerable distance across the prairies. If we found one at an appropriate height, we would use them as hurdles for the horses to jump. Fortunately, the animals never caught a hoof or fell. Some rods that crossed draws we could ride under. We also used the roads as racetracks. Here, too, Anne usually beat me, as my big, part-workhorse, Irish, was no match for her half-thoroughbred, Zipper.

I can't remember ever listening to a weather report on the radio (if there were any then). Grandma sometimes admonished me, "Watch the weather, and don't get caught in a storm." From hilltops we could look to Glacier Park and the Rocky Mountains 50 miles to the west, so we could generally see a storm coming and head for home to beat it.

On one of our trips, we rode further onto the reservation and played more than planned, for all of a sudden it was almost sunset. We knew we would be in trouble at our respective homes for getting back so late. We got across the river by dark, at about the same time it started raining. We had already taken our jackets off the ties behind the cantles and put them on, but they were soon soaked through, even my leather jacket. Rain dripped off our hats and oozed down our necks off our bandannas.

Anne couldn't help herself and started singing the Sons of the Pioneers' song, *Water*—"The night's so cool, and I'm a fool, each star's a pool of water..." The second time through, I joined in. Anne has a nice singing voice, so I listened to her the third time. As she kept singing it, it became less fun and more and more irritating. By the time we reached the barn, I already had quite enough of "cool, clear water." I don't think we had ever been so totally saturated. Even though it was summer, we were bone-chilled, and still had the bike ride back into town. I don't recall the dressing down I received, but it couldn't have been as bad as the ride.

Any time I hear that song, I'm back on a horse, in the dark, dripping water, shaking from the cold, and wanting to put a muzzle on my best pal.

FAMILY SAYINGS

My grandparents raised me, so I was probably more a child of the early 1900s. Grandma baked our bread, made noodles, soap, dried vegetables, and of course canned fruits and vegetables. I learned all the old adages of "a stitch in time saves nine," and "a penny saved is a penny earned."

A special language, or at least phrases, develops in families. Some are extracted from the common language of the nation or area. I received all kinds of dire warnings.

When pouting or angry, I was admonished, "Your face will freeze that way if you're not careful."

"You'll grow a long nose if you lie."

"If you go out in this snow and cold you'll grow an icicle on your nose."

"If you keep falling and bruising yourself, you'll get bone cancer." I didn't know what cancer was, but realized it must've been bad stuff.

"Don't go outside with your hair wet like that. You'll catch your death of cold."

"Get outside, and air some of the stink off you."

Grandma used to tell me she was out of breath. That I could understand, from running, or playing hard, or just silly laughing. She also would say she was "short of breath." That I couldn't understand until now.

I thought Ex-Lax was the best chocolate I had ever tasted but Gram told me. "It isn't candy. You stay out of it. It's medicine and too much will kill you." Now they have to package pills and other medicines in three layers of childproof deterrents to keep kids out of them, but back then we obeyed warnings, especially all the death threats.

If I fussed about something too much, I heard, "Don't pick a scab on your nose." I was also warned, "Don't get behind yourself," to get me to stop and think out the situation.

"What you don't carry in your head you have to carry in your feet," puzzled me for a long time.

Nipples on a dog or cat we called "buttons on its vest."

People called the big tan grasshoppers with yellow or red wings "witch doctors." I've never found another place that uses that name for them.

After my first puppy died: "The disease (distemper) stays in the ground for years, so you can't have another dog." This quelled my begging for a time.

Grandpa's observation of some skin-tight Levi's I wore in high school, "Those pants fit too soon."

Later when I was going off to college, Grandpa warned me not to become an educated fool. He also told me to remember that an education is one thing that can never be taken away from you.

Grandma would comment, "I forgot what I was going to say. It must've been a lie." She also said, "When you dream of someone dead, they have come back to visit you in your sleep."

She talked about people who had a child in less than nine months after they married, "They went to church before the bell rang." My cousins worked in the Cut Bank oil fields in the mid-50s to put themselves through college, and lived with Gram and Gramps. He warned them, "Don't go stirrin' up a puddin' with any of the girls you date." These were warnings from experience, as Uncle Bob was born seven months after my grandparents' marriage. Experience is the best teacher.

When Aunt Joe's temper flared, Gram said, "Joe's red hair is crackling today." (Yes, she spelled it Joe. Her given name was Juanita.)

And I can still hear Joe reminding me when I drove out on a trip, "Keep it between the fence posts, kid." That went back to the two-lane highways, usually fenced on either side. In bad road conditions, the fences were good guides.

Mom too had pearls of wisdom like "I'm so mad, I could spit tacks."

"She's so good butter wouldn't melt in her mouth."

A bit worse, "She's so nice she wouldn't say shit if her mouth was full of it."

My cousins complained, "I'm so hungry I could eat the rear end out of a skunk." That thought still nauseates me. I much prefer "He's so hungry he thinks his throat is cut."

One of Uncle Bob's favorite expressions was, "He's as busy as a cat trying to bury crap on a marble floor." He taught us "poohsapoot," which is the Blackfoot Indian word for "come here." He also used it as "hurry up" when we lagged behind. When we complained of a chore or put it off, Uncle Bob would ask, "Are you crippled, handcuffed, hog-tied, or shackled?" We always said "No" and got with it.

Gram must have learned some German as a child. "Was ist los?" and the reply, "Nichts ist los." Or "What's happening?" "Nothing." Occasionally Gram would get angry and say, 'Oh, scheise," which I was not allowed to repeat. "Wie geht es Ihnen?" What Gram meant was, "What are you doing?" But actually, the phrase means, "How do you do?"

When scolding me she'd tell me "schimelstu" or "schamelich." Maybe they were Pennsylvania Dutch for "shame on you." I heard those a lot. This was the extent of our foreign language learning at home.

I don't know who taught us Pig Latin, but we could speak it as rapidly as regular talk. "Ancay ouyay elltay atway I-ay asay?"

We also had favorite chants, like, "Liar, liar, pants on fire, nose as long as a telephone wire." "I see London, I see France, I see Jane Doe's underpants." "Oh, my gracious, oh my soul, there goes Jane Doe down the hole!"

Tongue twisters were fun. We challenged each other to say them faster and faster until our tongues did twist. "I slit a sheet, a sheet I slit, upon a slitted sheet I sit." was one of our favorites because of the bad word our tongues slipped into. I wonder, do kids still say them?

I'm not sure if it was a tongue twister that Mom would say—a chant taking someone's name, "Tessie, kadessie, carip-a-tip-a-Tessie. Tee leg-ged, toe leg-ged, two-leg-ged Tessie." Such nonsense could occupy a few minutes of idle time before we bounded off to more physical activity.

Knock-knock jokes were popular too. One of Mom's I remember is:

"Knock knock."

"Who's there?"

"Tarzan."

"Tarzan who?"

"Tarzan stripes forever."

Dear reader, if you are one of those who thrive on political correctness, please skip the next two paragraphs. This is history, the way it was in the 1930s and 1940s. There was no rancor in the sayings. They were just what we learned.

Brazil nuts were called, "Nigger toes." A large, roundish stone in a gravel road was a "Nigger head," as was big log floating upright in a lake with only a foot or so sticking out of the water. "Sweating like a Nigger at election." "There's a Nigger in the woodpile." "He acts like he's Nigger rich." All these were everyday expressions, completely without any meanness. We also went "Nigger fishing," which involved putting bait on a hook, weights just above it, and a float two or three feet up the line. We then tossed it out in the lake or pond, secured the pole at an angle, so we could sit and read or go off for a short time, later checking to see if a fish had taken the bait.

To select who would be "it" or divide into teams, we used the following chant: (Some American versions of this rhyme use "nigger" instead of "tiger.")

"Eeny, meeny, miny, moe,
Catch a tiger by the toe;
If he hollers let him go,
Eeny meeny, miny, moe."

Sometimes we added, "I choose you," if a chant ended up on someone we didn't want on our team.

The only Negroes we saw were waiters and porters on the passenger trains. I never connected those men to our sayings. Now, Nigger has become "the N word" on a par with "the F word." I wonder what the next unspeakable word will become: Muslim? Prostitute? Congressman?

A poem that I often heard from Grandpa when we kids became too boisterous:

"Too much of joy is sorrowful
So, cares must need a bound.
The vine that bears too many flowers
Will trail upon the ground."

It startles me that I am probably the only one now who remembers all this. Some is best forgotten. I don't understand the dress, fads, or lingo of these new generations. Tattoos and body piercing that we used to see in National Geographic on primitive tribes are common now. We can never go back to a quieter, slower, nicer time. I do hope families still have little traditions and sayings unique to them or the community.

**Part 2
1950s & 1960s**

GRANDPA'S DEATH

My beloved Grandpa Pat died when I was 22. For some reason, Mom and Grandma had not told me that he had rectal cancer. He had called it "bleeding piles," but not to me. Mom finally told me that Grandma was worn out washing sheets every day, because he bled on the bed nightly. He had been in the Cut Bank hospital for this, and was finally taken to Fort Harrison Veterans' Hospital near Helena, Montana.

Surgery was scheduled for Monday, and Grandma, Mom, and George, her husband, prepared to go down to be there when he came out of the anesthetic. Grandpa called them the night before, and said not to come as the surgery had been postponed. Late Monday morning his doctor called, wondering where they were and to tell them the operation was not successful. He said, "Mr. Micken is full of cancer and dying from heart failure." They did not get there before he died.

I have wondered about his reason for lying to them, perhaps he didn't want two hysterical women around, or he didn't want them worrying. At any rate, I am certain he felt he would not live through the surgery.

At his insistence, I had gone to Cheney, Washington to summer school as planned. I had wanted to stay home, so

I could visit him and be close, but he insisted that an education should come first. He had only completed fourth grade, which was not uncommon in the late 1800s.

Very early the morning he died, I dreamt of him. I dreamed I was in bed there at the college, and he came into the room, sat on the edge of my bed, and talked to me. I noticed his left hand had all five fingers. He had lost his thumb and forefinger in an accident in 1925. I don't recall all he said, except at the end, "Everything will be all right." For some reason I felt frightened of him, then it felt like an electric shock went through me, and I wakened. Later that morning, George called to tell me of Grandpa's death.

Although I had a car, I decided to go home by train because of emotional meltdown. I notified my various instructors, packed, and caught the late train to Cut Bank. Optimistically I took books and notebooks so I could study, but didn't open them.

I wrote this on the train when returning to Cut Bank for his funeral.

JUNE 1955

Tick tock
And the hands of the clock
On the wall
Tell me a minute is past.

Tock tick
He was only sick,
But an error
Of words—sick to death.

Tock tock
Hands never stop
In their trip
Around hours and days.

Tick tick
Their patient trick
Is to trap you,
Then run you out dead

Tick tick tock
Is the pace of the clock
Running fast
'Till a life is passed.

Our small clan gathered: Grandma, their two sons and their wives, Mom, George, and Grandma's and Grandpa's six grandchildren. There was a Masonic funeral and a military graveside service. Many of his friends were in attendance. Grandma had received a letter of apology from Governor J. Hugo Aronson that he was tied up in meetings and could not attend the funeral. He did send flowers. He had taken time twice to visit Grandpa in the hospital in Helena, giving him a handful of change each time, so he could "call home and buy candy." Grandpa fairly glowed when telling me about it when I visited before leaving for Cheney.

At graveside, I mainly remember Grandma almost fainting at the first shot of the 21-gun salute. To this day, when I hear that on TV or at a funeral, I'm immediately standing by the casket at Crown Hill Cemetery, crying.

Even then, I felt solace in writing poetry, and so did on the return trip to school.

JUNE 1955

Softly spider, spin your web,
Weave it of black silk for the dead.
Weep and wilt, you tossing flowers,
Crumple in sorrow, for Death has ours.
The house's master died this day.
Cry, you poplars, droop and sway.
The sun will not rise, nor stars come out.
Hearts are empty, joy's in rout.

But the spider beautifully spins her web
Of sheer white silk, for she's not dead.
The tossing flowers swell and bloom,
To live again come next June.
The poplars raise their leaves for sun,
And thank their god for days to come.
Sunrise's splendor lifts the clouds—
A glimpse of Heaven beyond the shrouds.

The spider's eggs will hatch this fall.
The flowers' seeds to spring will thrall
To grow and bloom in colors bold.
The poplars' leaves will turn to gold,
Then drop to shield the grasses' sleep.
Spring rains bring life up from the deep,
And so the cycles ever turn.
Life moves on, we have to learn.

Lori at Blue Lake with Dunkel

AXOLOTL

In 1963, I took a year off teaching to work on a master's degree in zoology at Montana State College in Bozeman (now Montana State University).

A spring herpetology class field trip to the Ennis/Virginia City area gave me the idea for my fieldwork. Dr. Cliff Davis, the instructor and also my advisor, drove our small class to Blue Lake, the highest of the Axolotl Lakes at an elevation of 7780 feet. A dirt road left the top of Virginia City/Ennis pass. It meandered across the grassy hills, took a breathtaking descent over a basalt rubble field, straight down to more rolling hills with scattered patches of evergreens.

Blue Lake is small, about 1000 feet long and 200 feet wide, a narrow ellipse set up against a sheer basalt cliff. There are no inlet or outlet streams, just seepage through the rubble rock. Swarms of axolotls (amphibians) surrounded a huge boulder in the south end of the lake.

Axolotls are the neotonic form of the tiger salamander. Neotony is retaining the larval form in a sexually mature salamander. Three sets of long, red, feathery external gills adorn the neck, and a translucent fin runs from the head down the middle of the back to around the tail. In metamorphosis these are absorbed, lungs formed, and the skin's mud color becomes pale green with spots of darker green.

The week after our field trip, I conferred with Dr. Davis on a thesis topic, suggesting a survey of the small lakes and ponds in the area around Blue Lake, and to propose a hypothesis for their neotony, discovery by Europeans in 1864 in Mexico. Dr. Davis accepted my plan.

In mid-June 1964, I obtained permission from the Bureau of Land Management to set up a simple camp above Blue Lake. On my first trip there, it took all my courage to drive down that one stretch of road over the rockslide. It was only a 28-foot drop in elevation, but a steep, straight line of road to the bottom.

For the camp, I dug a fire pit and a trench latrine, and collected dead wood for fires. My International Harvester Scout became my bedroom, using a plywood sheet laid across the flat cover of the wheel wells and the folded down back seat. Dunkel, my dachshund, accompanied me and acted as a protector.

The only bad thing about the fieldwork was a plague of P.A. flies: pointed abdomen or pointed ass flies. The black plastic tarp over the woodpile sounded like a heavy rain from the flies hitting it. The heat must have attracted them. Their bite is vicious and creates a red, itchy lump that remains active for weeks. They didn't seem to bother Dunkel. Late afternoons, I sprayed the Scout's interior with insecticide so by bedtime all insects had died.

If silence is golden, I had platinum. The soft rustling of the evergreens in a night breeze was generally the only sound. I didn't often take time to enjoy the wild beauty and solitude of the area.

I spent my days in fishing boots, wading, bent over to shade the swampy-smelling water of the 15 lakes and ponds in the five square mile area around Blue Lake. I collected and identified the plants and animals in each. A net enabled me to catch anything of interest. Primarily

I searched for more axolotls. Each lake or pond seemed to have a specialty organism. One pond had hundreds of snails, another droves of scuds, a small crustacean.

A higher lake had an active beaver colony. One day hiking on the trail by this lake, I frightened a beaver dragging an aspen sapling. It dropped the food and hustled to the lake. Feeling badly, I dragged the young tree to the lake for it.

Only twice did I see other people in the area. One was the rancher who leased the BLM land for his cattle. Fortunately, the cattle never ventured to the Blue Lake area.

The other encounter was more exciting. With the Scout jolting down the rockslide hill, I glanced up and saw two people in the distance, walking away from me. They must have heard the vehicle, as they started running toward me, screaming for help and waving. Driving up to them, I found a nearly hysterical, middle-aged couple, both in tears.

Gasping, they said, "Would you give us a ride?"

"Of course." The man immediately clambered in back on the plywood with all my gear.

"What are you doing up here and on foot?" Their casual street clothes and shoes weren't for hiking in this country.

They pieced together their story, talking over each other. "We flew into Bozeman, rented a car, and started for Virginia City."

"We're from Los Angeles."

"A man at the gas station in Ennis told us about a shortcut on a dirt road to Virginia City that was passable but slow, and went through some beautiful country."

"We decided to take the adventure." She shook her head.

"We passed the fish hatchery where the pavement ended. The dirt road looked pretty good," the man said, "but it was soon only two ruts. We drove through what looked like a shallow mud puddle, but it was deep and we got stuck.

"He decided we could walk, as it seemed we must be nearly to Virginia City."

"There are so many little roads here…"

"We didn't know which to take or which way the town lies." She started crying again.

I broke in. "The way you were walking would've taken you into the Gravelly Range. Virginia City is about six miles that way," I pointed, "and Ennis is about the same distance east."

The woman paled, "We never would have made it. We could have died."

"Yes, that's possible: exposure, dehydration, exhaustion."

"Wild animals," he added. "Aren't you afraid to be up here alone?"

I laughed. "Heavens no. This Scout is my bedroom, quite secure against any dangers while I'm asleep. Dunkel, my dachshund here, is my alarm and guardian."

Her hands covered her heart. "You're brave. Aren't you afraid of being injured or attacked by wild animals?"

"Those things never entered my mind."

We visited on the way into Ennis to the Pharmacy Restaurant where civilization would surround them. Of course, I refused their offer of money. They asked for my address so they could let me know how the rest of their trip went and that they were home safe. Her farewell statement, "You are our hero," warmed me.

I returned to my camp, smiling all the way at their good luck and mine. Not often one has a chance to be a hero.

About three weeks later, a small package from my lost Californians arrived in the mail. It contained a beautiful, red enamel and gold lizard two inches long. She wrote she'd searched all over for a salamander, but this lizard was as close as she could get.

Back at camp, the day of the tourists, I set out the five-gallon can of water for cooking and washing and a cooler chest of food. Even heroes have to work, so I walked around the lake. At the shallow, northern end, I found that eggs had recently been laid on twigs that had fallen in the lake. The eggs are gelatinous, transparent, and sticky. Algae already had started to adhere to the surface. I measured, counted, and made sketches to augment the pictures taken. That's the only area of the lake where the axolotls laid eggs. I returned there daily, taking notes and observing with a hand lens. I took some eggs and twigs with me to town, to continue observations, plus searching out and collecting newly laid ones at the lake.

Unfortunately, the larvae are cannibalistic as are the adults of their young. Of 54 eggs and young studied, only three lived through the summer in the lab. I fed them insect larvae, crustaceans, and pieces of angleworm. These captives had grown from three-eighths inch at hatching to over three inches by the end of August,

My adventures in driving around Blue Lake area proved more exciting than the fieldwork. One day, on a road new to me, there was a loud scrape and the front wheels dropped a bit. I stopped to look under the vehicle. It had a skid plate of heavy iron from behind the front bumper to back beyond the front axle, protecting the engine and oil pan. A large pointed rock now set just back of the skid plate. I couldn't drive backward because of the plate and was afraid to move forward for fear of damaging the axle or differential. Conundrum.

A theory formed. To get the offending rock back under the skid plate, I collected a pile of big flattish rocks, jacked up one front wheel, placed rocks under it, and then did the same with the other. It worked beautifully, and I was on my way, after unstacking the stones and distributing them about.

On one trip out, driving up the dreaded steep section of rubble rock, I heard another scrape but kept going. The engine continued to run smoothly; all gauges were on normal. Everything was fine until I drove down a small hill and found I had no brakes. The minor scrape had punctured the brake line.

I was at the top of the Virginia City Hill, six miles down a steep, winding road to Ennis. I hoped my gears would hold me in four-wheel-drive low gear.

Creeping out onto the highway after turning on my lights (hazard lights hadn't been invented, at least not for the Scout). I kept one wheel on the gravel and at intervals turned right to slow even further or stop. I don't recall how long it took to reach the garage in Ennis, but my arms and shoulders ached, and my hands felt molded to the steering wheel.

Fortunately, the mechanic could fix it in a short time. At first, he seemed skeptical of my story of how I got there, but I convinced him.

Before going home for bath and bed, I went to my office on campus. Carrying the plastic bag with eggs and the five-gallon can of lake water up the three flights of stairs took several rest-stops and about did me in.

My study extended over two summers, plus library research and taking notes on the hatchlings. For several years, I visited the lake in summer to check on the axolotls. Besides writing two papers for the Montana Academy of Sciences, the Montana Fish and Game (now Fish, Wildlife, and Parks) invited me to present a talk on my research at their state meeting.

I had reached only tentative conclusions about the axolotls, namely that the short "growing season" held up tissue growth of reproductive organs or of hormones, preventing maturation of the sex organs and development of the accompanying physical changes of losing the external gills and fin.

It has been nearly 60 years since adventuring into Blue Lake country. I wonder if I'd have the courage to drive down that awful rock hill and hike into all the lakes and ponds. Mostly, I wonder if the axolotls still swim there. It remains BLM land, so the wilderness is preserved. I hope nothing, no one, has somehow eradicated those creatures. Such a wonderful community needs to be preserved and marveled at.

DUNKEL AND OTHER DACHSHUNDS

I started teaching in 1952. I spent my summers in college or working Scout camps, so I went without a dog until 1960 when I decided to spend the summer building a cabin. Aunt Joe and Uncle Bob had neighbors who raised dachshunds. I purchased a little black, smooth-coat puppy for $25 from them.

When I went to get him, I dressed up in my good wool saddle pants, I guess as of way to make myself seem more affluent. I put a heavy towel on the passenger seat for the pup and started to drive off. He immediately crawled onto my lap and soaked my pants, perhaps as a way of marking me as his own. Of course, he had to have a German name, so I chose Dunkel, meaning dark.

Dunkel was a somber little puppy, sleeping a lot and playing with sticks while I worked on cabin building. He slept in the car at night, but by day I put him on his own recognizance in the woods and beginning cabin. One afternoon, it dawned on me I hadn't seen him for a while. He didn't come when I called so I searched up at the car, under the cabin, and through the woods. I finally went down to the lake, and found him caught in a V of branches, struggling to get on shore. He never took himself to the lake alone again.

That fall, once school started, I brought him with me in the car when the weather was nice. I took my students on several walking field trips, and he went along, so they all knew him.

I decided to take a year off teaching to attend Montana State College in Bozeman and work on a master's degree in zoology. Of course, Dunkel went to school, too. I bicycled the half-mile across town to campus, taking him in the bike basket. He attended class and labs with me. Such things weren't allowed later on.

A dachshund's vocation is hunting badgers. Lacking those, I took him grouse hunting. He watched when a bird flew and where it dropped. I had to be fast in catching up with him to keep him from eating my kill. I always gave him the heart, liver, and kidneys when cleaning them.

One time three grouse flew up at once. He somehow kept track of where they landed, ran to the base of the trees, and started barking. I shot those two, also. He believed that whenever I shot, I had killed something and would cast out searching for the body even when I missed. Just seeing me get out the shotgun put him in paroxysms of joy.

To augment my vanishing money for college, I substitute taught in Bozeman and Livingston. This necessitated missing some classes and labs. The only makeup lab I recall was in herpetology on poisonous snakes. Dr. Davis gave me the keys to Lewis Hall and the lab on the third floor.

Except for Dunkel, I was the only one in the building at 7 p.m. Spooky.

Dr. Davis left the huge jars of snakes out on the floor for me. Boom-slang, pit vipers, cobra, cottonmouth, black mamba, sea snake; all floating in 5-gallon glass vats, awaiting my inspection. They were uniform formaldehyde brown to tan. "They are dead," I reminded myself, "pickled for years, the colors leached out they've been dead so long."

It took all my courage and mental grit to dip in and pull out a North American poisonous snake. There were no plastic gloves available, so I reached in barehanded and lifted out—was it a rattler, or a sidewinder? I got out the key, counted nose scales and looked for "horns" of scales on top of the head. Rattler.

Next was a cottonmouth, and on and on. The cobra's hood had been flared out to show the now vague marking on the back of it. By 10 o'clock, I'd finish North and South America, Africa, and Asia poisonous snakes. I don't remember if Europe had any, probably didn't, following the example of the Irish. My fingertips were all badly puckered and felt numb from the formaldehyde. Dunkel had moved across the room to sleep to get some relief from the smell.

Of course, Dunkel accompanied me on my field trips to the Axolotl Lakes out of Virginia City. Poor boy picked up range mites and lost his lovely black hair, except on his head, feet, and lower legs. The medication from the vet was a sick-chartreuse paste that had to be smeared all over him. He was a pitiful sight: a nearly hairless, greenish specimen from outer space. Eventually the mites were killed off, and he regained his glossy, black fur coat.

Another dachshund vocation is digging. When I moved to the country, he dug his paws raw. I tried putting socks, then booties, on him, but he would tear them off and resume his digging for pocket gophers and any other underground critters. Eventually the newness wore off and with frozen ground, he retired to being a housedog again.

Unfortunately, he developed heart trouble and died at only ten years old.

Somehow, my students in advanced biology learned of his death. The girls in the class chipped together and bought me a tiny dachshund puppy for Christmas. Those were students that I had taught in junior high and in sophomore biology, so we were well acquainted. I named the little mite, only as long as my hand, Blitzkrieg: Lioness of Judah.

She grew up to be 12 pounds of spunk and companionship, living up to her name, as she considered herself queen of all she surveyed. She was not a hunter but did love to be carried along when I rode horseback. I was careless in checking on her when she was out one night, and she disappeared. I rode my horse out searching for her the next day and found her body. Apparently, an owl had snatched her up and couldn't fly far with her. Fortunately, it had not eaten on her. She had lived only three years.

That same year my former biology girls told me where they had purchased Blitz. The breeder had had another litter and I bought Schatten, German for "shadow." And indeed, she was my shadow for three weeks short of 19 years. She loved to grouse hunt and also come with me fishing. I had to be careful when landing a fish, as she would instantly attack it, bent on eating it. She really didn't like to get in the water, but if I crossed the stream and stayed on the other side, she would grimly swim over to me.

Mousing was another of her skills, and she kept the house and even my car clear of them.

Up in Axolotl country, I winged a sage hen and she tore after it. I followed a trail of feathers down the hill to where she had finally gotten a hold of the bird and not just its tail. German stubbornness. As she grew older, I would carry her in a backpack when hunting and put her out to get the grouse. It was a long, happy, productive relationship. She was the last of my German phase, and I switched to the Welsh corgi.

NIGHT OWLS

Two young great horned owls entertained me one night in the yard light's circle in front of the house. They had the smooth faces of helmeted knights, almost white, but from there down, things became disorganized, and their adolescence showed in loose, frowsy, disheveled feathers.

They would ruffle their feathers, then shake them, but to no avail. Everything remained messy. At long intervals they would stretch tall, scratch, groom, then stretch again. Their heads did the typical owl turn, seemingly in a full circle. Usually they were alert but did yawn and look drowsy with half-open eyes, as though wishing to be back in the nest again. A big white foot would slowly move out, flex, then the wing on the same side would be stretched, too. Or a foot would slowly reach up to scratch its beak with one claw.

Their main business, though, was hunting. They did an odd bobbing and weaving of their heads before taking off, as though they were trying to sight in on something on the ground. They would move from the metal fence posts, to the jackleg fence, to the road, to the lawn, to the pasture, and to the yard light post. Then one would be silently gone, suddenly re-materializing as part of a wooden fence post with big, taloned feet declaring it wasn't really wood.

Sometimes both would fly down to the ground at once, working beak-to-beak, then side-by-side, like a pair of huge, vicious chickens. What they were eating I could not see, but they would run along the ground and grasp something in a talon, usually the right one, and eat it. Many bats were out that night, also, eating the moths and other insects attracted to the light. I assumed the owls, too, were dining on bugs.

Much of the time they were solemn and silent, looking often at each other as though seeking approval. They would call, too, a babyish-sounding "kreek," which I thought would frighten prey into immobility. Although they were babies, they were also killers. The next day, I found the remnants of a grouse with only feathers, wings, and legs left. I wondered if it had been owled.

Later that summer, I noticed some sort of mass near the top of the power pole. It turned out to be a dead owl. Apparently on takeoff or landing, there had been a fatal connection of a wing or foot on the power line. The loss of such a wonderful creature was heartbreaking. Owls should get to grow old and die a natural death, for they are few in number.

HUNTER

Death sits in velvet silence,
Fringed wings furled.
Chereep! sounds hoarse across the meadow.
The great yellow eyes search.
Ears are tuned fine for any sound.

Chereep! again and again the call.
There is no malice, no bloodthirsty lust.
The search is for sustenance only.

Hush, a slight stir, soft feet move
Quickly along the ground.
Without a sound, the vast wings spread,
And the body lifts free.
A noiseless glide.
A puff of dust by waving grasses
As sharp talons
Strike their goal in a sweep of soundless skill.

The mouse is dead.
The owl will live.

Grandpa Pat Micken

AN OPPOSABLE THUMB

A couple weeks ago, I managed to bash my thumb, not enough to blacken the thumbnail, but lower, enough to make it very sore, swollen, and almost useless for everyday tasks. I never thought how much the left thumb is used. It is needed to button a shirt, open jars, pull up panties, socks, and jeans, hold a fork to cut meat, tie shoelaces, and many other things.

My grandfather had been in a horrible accident at 49 years old, in 1925. His left thumb and forefinger were crushed under a 125-ton roller used in a dragline, building roads near Cut Bank. He told me the men he was working with put him in the rear seat of a car and drove across the prairies 15 miles to Browning, the nearest town. He said he regained consciousness and saw his hand was bleeding heavily, so he slowed the blood flow by grabbing his wrist. The doctor amputated Grandpa's thumb and forefinger to the wrist and stitched the layers with black suture.

One of those black stitches partially worked its way out of the scar when I was five. He asked me to pull it out after he cut the skin a bit. Pride of being helpful kept me from being squeamish.

Workman's Comp hadn't come to Montana, so he had to sell his house to provide for his family of five in the weeks when he was unable to work. There was no physical therapy available then, either, so he had to figure out ways to utilize the three remaining fingers.

I can remember him turning the radio knob between ring and middle fingers. He could also hold an apple with those three fingers and his palm, while quartering it with a knife. When he bought me a jackknife at age nine, he demonstrated how to safely open and close it, again holding it in his left-hand remnant while he lifted the blade with his right fingers.

He had to wear mittens in winter rather than gloves. Regardless of the weather he often pulled them off when working outside to manipulate objects better.

He was the entire city water department in our small town—reading meters, supervising laying lines of water and sewage to new houses, sending water samples to the state, and whatever else was required of the job.

I never heard Grandpa complain about trading the homestead (which later had three oil wells on it) for a house in town, or about selling that house because of the accident, or about losing part of his hand. In fact, he generally enjoyed life, often saying, "I'm happy to have a roof over my head, three square meals a day, and a good job."

After reminiscing a bit, I have quit whining about my sore thumb.

HUMMINGBIRDS

My grandparents' house had a wide porch in front with an almost three-foot solid board wall topped by a foot-wide plank. Gramps had made two rectangular wood planters to set on them so Gram could have even more flowers.

She bought some plants from Pete Unger who had a greenhouse. He spoke with a heavy Italian accent and called one flower Gram bought "snap-a-da-drags." She also bought petunias from him to put in her porch planters. Most of her plants she grew from seeds from her flowers from the year before. Some seeds she collected from the plants in East Glacier at the Great Northern Hotel flowerbeds.

When young, I thought we had hummingbirds at the petunias, but someone told me they were hummingbird moths (white-lined sphinx moths, I later learned). They looked like hummingbirds to me, although I had only seen pictures of the birds. I doubt, with the lack of trees and shrubs for nesting and few flower gardens, that there were any of the birds in Cut Bank back in the 1930s and '40s. But the moths were fun to watch, hovering and softly buzzing at the flowers in late afternoon and evening.

Then, finally, in the lush flower gardens at East Glacier, I saw a real hummingbird feeding on the towering blue larkspur plants that formed the center of the flowerbeds. I was enchanted. The wings were such a blur as to be invisible. The tiny bird didn't perch, but hung suspended in front of the blossoms, moving in jerks from one to another, drinking from each. I watched until it buzzed off.

Now, many years later, I put up feeders on the patio at my house near Livingston and at my cabin in western Montana. I have the same two species at both places—calliope and rufus.

Last summer, a male black-chinned hummingbird came to the patio at the house. A feisty little guy, he chased my resident birds away, declaring his territory. He perched by the flower barrel five feet from the feeder much of the time. The next day he was gone.

At the cabin, I used to have three feeders and had to fill them every two or three days, as there would be as many as nine hummingbirds at a time. Now, one feeder lasts a week, and I am lucky to see two or three at once. I believe the reduction in the birds' numbers is due to the Forest Service's drastic thinning of the woods in the area. There is no longer a forest, as they felled about two-thirds of the trees six years ago. For one thing, the remnant forest is 3° to 5° warmer than at my cabin where the trees were not cut. Of course, this makes it drier over there, too. Yes, the forest will return, but I won't live long enough to see if the birds come back.

Several times I have had the thrill of actually holding one of these tiny creatures. Each flew through the open door of my entry shed at the cabin. I gently caught them as they fought to get out through the glass. They weigh nothing more than a dandelion seed head. I released them immediately, not wanting to further stress them.

The males sometimes fight their reflections on the windows, tweeping and diving in a perfect fury over the reflection.

Hummingbirds stay in Montana from around May 1 to around September 1, then fly south for the remaining seven months of the year. It's a bit lonely after they leave, but a perfect delight when they return.

Now, it has been over 70 years since I've seen a hummingbird moth. I wouldn't mind a sighting to return me to that childish wonder, but the real hummers are even more of a delight.

CHANGES AT THE LAKE

October is a quiet time. There isn't much to watch at the lake but the lake itself, sparkling in beginning waves: a repeating pattern of swells and troughs like a marcel hairdo. Reflections of the mountains and trees are erased. The wind increases. The waves, now hurrying to shore in bigger crests and basins, hit the boat by the dock with a slap, slap, and thunk. The only other sounds are creaking and sighing of trees in the wind, and occasional calls of crows, camp robbers, and chickadees.

All other birds have fled: the loons to California's ocean bays, hummingbirds and swallows to Mexico, the mergansers to the West Coast, red-winged blackbirds, swallows, great blue herons and sandhill cranes journey even further south.

First to leave in late August are the hummingbirds. I wonder that they can fly 2500 miles when only two-and-three-quarter inches long. It's a good thing they don't fret, as I do, about the distance. It's not quite so miraculous that the larger birds can make their trips. One of the last to leave is this year's loon chick. It hatched as a black, fuzzy, tennis ball-sized baby three and a half months ago. Now full grown, it is a strapping eight pounds with a wingspan of nearly four feet. Its parents left two or three weeks before, and the baby must find its own way to the ocean, hopefully ganging up with other young loons.

The lake is dying, filling in from every edge. The insect life is dying too. Both dragonfly species are reduced in numbers, also their cousins the damselflies. In summer I see fewer and fewer giant water beetles, water striders, whirligig beetles, and flies. The numbers of minnows and small suckers, also, have dwindled. In but two years the shallow water at the south side of the dock has grown thick with cattails. Pondweed is choking off the water at the dock's end.

The lake's greatest depth is 35 feet, so it will take many years to fill. Just a small pond will be left there in 100 or 200 years. The cabin will be a pile of rubble or long since burned in a wildfire. Looking into the future is insane. Tomorrow is too far to look in the crystal ball.

"Used to be," has become my mantra. At the lake's edge, there used to be sundews we fed ants. Bitterns used to nest in the massive growth of cattails at the lake's ends. Those have died out, and the cattail area is semi-dry land with grasses, sedges, and a few alders growing in the new soil. So, the bitterns are gone. Where once we could take a raft between the cattail swamp and forest, there now is land and a growth of bushes. The freshwater sponges are dying out. There used to be a plethora of toads and Columbia spotted frogs. Now, seeing one is an event.

I don't like change. I want there always to be a beaver lodge at the lake's edge with fireweed growing on it, and barred owls calling in the night, and ospreys and loons fishing by day.

The tiny Pacific tree frogs, red-sided garter snakes, long-toed salamanders, mosquitoes, cattails and yellow pond lilies are still here.

And so am I, listening to the quiet of autumn and memories.

Lori on Warlock, August 1971

WARLOCK, THE LAST HORSE

While in high school, I had three horses at different times: Snooks, an old pinto mare; Irish, a huge sorrel gelding with white mane and tail and four tall white socks; and Shamrock, a black filly with flaxen mane and tail. Then I was horseless for 13 years.

When driving east of Bozeman, just beyond Bridger Canyon, I noticed a big brown pinto in a field. On the return trip, I drove down to the house by the pasture and asked about the horse. His owner said he was six years old, green broke, a gelding. I agreed to buy him for $150. Martin said he could not deliver him as his one attempt at trailering him failed. The gelding kicked the old wood horse trailer to pieces when he shut the tailgate. So I decided I'd ride him home the 12 miles. Martin offered to loan me his saddle and warned me the horse was deathly afraid of water, as he had nearly drowned in an irrigation ditch as a small colt. That didn't concern me; there was no water to cross. Also, he warned, the gelding had never been away from that home pasture or his mother, nor had he been on pavement.

I had driven back streets through Bozeman to find the best route through town. Home lay on a quiet road four miles south of town. We navigated the highway pavement without a problem, passed the stockyards, and kept to side streets with only an occasional "wufff" and shy. He seemed to be enjoying the adventure as much as I. At the railroad tracks, he balked. Apparently to his horse eyes and memory, it was water, deadly water, fearsome water. I guided him back and forth across the road, turned around to reapproach, and finally got him to cross. His gigantic leap would have cleared a six-foot stream.

My housemate, Marga, followed us part time, slowing traffic on the highway and through town with her red convertible. Finally, the horse and I reached home, both exhausted, road weary, and unnerved. I had also decided on a name for him—Warlock—and became totally infatuated with him.

Warlock and I worked on neck reining, going through the various gaits, and starting and stopping. Not being able to afford a saddle, I had purchased a saddle pad with stirrups and cinch. It looked like a red and white, canvas, English saddle with a strap on the front for a handhold. That turned out to be a blessing as one day, leaving the house for a ride, he started bucking. The strap kept me on, but I came down on my hand and broke the little finger's end joint. Doc Clemons put it in a cast, but several days later, the pain became unbearable. He cut off the cast and found it had worn a sore right over the break. No more cast. I have a permanent bend and lump on the distal joint of the little finger. I'm always set to attend high tea, however, with the pinky finger out and bent.

In Warlock's early days with me, we did have a couple of other confrontations. As the summer progressed, he became hard to catch. I could generally run him into the narrow end of the pasture and corner him. One morning, he turned and charged me. I stood my ground and hit him across the face with the headstall. He skidded to a stop and literally sat a couple seconds. As he scrambled to get his hind legs under him, I looped the reins around his neck. After that, I had no trouble catching him.

Our rancher neighbor, Milt Schaplow, had plowed his field below our house. He gave me permission to cross it any time to ride to my friend, Helen Fechter's place, a mile below us. I rode down the field, paralleling the fence along the country road. Something spooked Warlock, or he thought a trot was too slow. He broke into a full run. I couldn't stop him so enjoyed the ride but did manage to bring him into a broad, wild turn. When he slowed, I kicked him into a gallop and kept running him up and down that furrowed dirt until he lathered. Then we sedately walked to Helen's. He never ran away again.

The previous year, we had purchased a Capp home that came as a lumber pile. The men who constructed the house were meticulous builders, checking every plank, beam, and 2 x 4 to be certain they were perfect. I kept the warped boards and built Warlock a barn with those discards. Most weren't too bad, so it went up relatively plumb and level. I put in two windows, set on either side, and an opening in the back between the mangers. I made a half door, which opened with a pulley to access the hay in back.

One day, I discovered a dead deer near the barn. She had hung up on the barbwire fence. I got her untangled and down on the ground so she could be dragged off up the hill into the woods. Warlock wouldn't get to within 15 feet of the dead animal. A longer rope solved the problem. He had never dragged anything before and was skittish, looking back and snorting when he caught the scent of her, sidestepping and tossing his head. Later, dragging a Christmas tree home was much easier. It didn't smell bad and weighed less.

Warlock and Marga's palomino mare, Chinook, moved with me to a place at the east side of the Bozeman Pass. That became their and my final home. Linda Stewart, my housemate, brought her mare, Whiskey, to the place, too. Warlock was delighted. He must have been "cut proud" as he acted like a stallion to his little herd of two mares.

When Whiskey foaled, we put Warlock in another pasture, fearful that he would injure the colt. He kept running the fence and screaming, so we put them together. He treated the filly as his own, staying with her when Whiskey went off to graze, nuzzling, telling deep secrets to her with rumblings. Never did he let her stray further from him than a few feet. Linda bred Whiskey a second time. Rimini and Warlock were not as close as he and Philly had been. Linda sold the colts, and Whiskey had to be put down because of foundering.

When Chinook died at 32 years old, Warlock searched and called and cried for three days, thundering all over the pasture. Eventually he gave up the search and settled into a lonely old age. He died peacefully at the side of the road near the house. We had been together 18 years.

ANCIENT HORSE

There stands Warlock,
Ancient horse, against
The sky of autumn.

He is a relic of my middle years.
We both are long of tooth,
Windswept, and unkempt.

He gained the highest hill
To collect the raw wind
And test his growing winter coat.

He is alone now. His mares
Have gone before him in death.
He knows this is his last winter.

AUTUMN COLORS

Rainbows have fallen to earth and covered the plants and ground in red, orange, yellow, green, and purple, plus every shade between. Blue we will have to take from the sky to complete the spectrum.

In the pine woods of western Montana, the forest floor is red and orange with huckleberry bushes. In individual leaves, however, are the real beauty of autumn's magic, each different and enchanting. Any one of them could be framed for a beautiful portrait of autumn's magnificence.

I grew up believing Jack Frost painted the leaves bright colors. Not so. He's a killer, turning the leaves brown or black, or if conditions are right, freezing them a permanent green.

The sorcery of color change is a molecule-by-molecule chemical conversion. I imagine tiny chemists in white coats traveling through the sap in the veins, carrying their beakers and stoppered vials into the cells. There they squeeze chlorophyll into their glassware and drop some magic substance from the vial in with it, shake well, and pour the substances into outgoing veins. This mix of water, nutrients, and sugar goes to the roots to be stored for next spring's growth. Then the little molecular chemists, with their jobs done, jump into the liquid as it sails down to the roots.

I imagine new scientists are in the leaves where the reds, oranges, and yellows are now visible. These colors blend and create every shade possible. The splendor of the bright colors is dismantled molecule by molecule, leaving only shades of brown.

Let's take just two huckleberry leaves as examples to describe: one is a soft reddish-orange with the main veins painted in pale chartreuse. The lower side is skin-colored with pale yellow veins. Now, in a few days, the colors deepen, and the veins are nearly invisible. A nearby leaf has darkened to a brownish purple with two spots of tangerine at its base and a rather surprising muddy green back. Every huckleberry leaf is different, but all have some line of the red and orange spectrum.

There are leaves of clear scarlet, some apricot, some burgundy, all with a lighter color on the underside layer of cells. Cottonwoods, mountain maple, willow, and honeysuckle turn shades of yellow, but it is the same chemical breakdown that produces these colors.

This sumptuous brocade is torn apart when the leaves fall, whether from breezes, animals brushing against them, or gravity. One by one they flutter, float and glide to earth. Or if there is a strong wind, they are torn off and blow free in legions.

Clement Moore wrote it best in his poem, *The Night Before Christmas*:

"As dry leaves that before the wild hurricane fly,
When they meet with an obstacle mount to the sky."

Properly pressed and dried, leaves retain their colors. After falling, though, they become one with the soil, turning brown. The cells themselves begin breaking apart. Sometimes the entire skeleton of veins may be left as a lacework when the other cells have disintegrated.

The grand view of whole trees and bushes covering an area in the colors of rainbows is indeed awesome, but a single leaf of the billions is just as wonderful. The miraculous autumn season is short; one leaf is incredible, the whole extravagance of nature to be cherished

PHANTASMAGORIA

In October, the gods of forest and mountains in western Montana have scattered trees of newly minted gold. In places, they poured forth whole mountains of them. This is the second magic of exploding colors, the first in cottonwoods, aspens, willows and other deciduous trees and shrubs. Those leaves have fallen to earth, brown and dead, leaving naked branches and twigs, their preparation for winter.

Here among the gloomy dark green pines, spruce, and fir, a molten glory runs across the land. The tamaracks, or larch, their less-lovely name, have lost their green and burst forth to light the woods. Perhaps the other needled trees are a bit aghast at their flamboyance? All summer the tamaracks blended in among their cousins. Now, suddenly, they become magnificent, proclaiming their difference and standing out like blazing firebrands. They are an Irish bull: a deciduous evergreen.

This flare of gold started nearly a month earlier, when there was but a hint of lighter green in the small, thin tamarack needles. Then daily, in tiny increments, lime green became chartreuse, became yellow, and darkened to gold: the gold of King Tut's treasures, the gold of Elizabeth's crown, the gold of the Vatican's wealth.

The tamarack needles fall, turning anything under them to gold leaf. For a time, the yellow brick road is everywhere. The forest, the lake, the roads are bedecked. There is what appears to be a mist of gold falling among the trees. Even I become spangled from the needles on my clothes and hair as I walk beneath them. Indeed, the mountain and forest gods are generous, letting us feast our eyes on more splendors in a week than Solomon had in his reign. Like sunset's colors, though, the time is brief to enjoy such a luxury of wealth. The tamaracks, too, become bare and the needled trees that marveled at their extravagance now can mock them and settle smug into a winter wrapped in evergreen.

Oh, it is better to joyfully ignite once a year for only awhile than to remain constantly predictable and not inspire awe.

Part 3
Final Home
45 Years

MISS BIOLOGY

For years I was "Miss Biology" to the town of Livingston: the high school biology teacher, fountain of knowledge botanical and zoological.

One day a messenger came from the office telling me to return a phone call in my free period. "Miss Micken," the frantic voice of a woman, "I've got a possum shut in the garage."

"That can't be. There are no opossums this far north."

"It's a possum. It has a bald tail. Can you come get it?"

"Well, yes, I guess so, after school's out."

"I don't want to have to kill it."

"Oh, don't do that. I can drive up now. Maybe this is someone's pet?"

She gave her address; I grabbed the department's live trap and a bottle of ether to tranquilize it if necessary. On the way to the north side hill I kept whistling "Possum in a Gum Tree."

On arrival at the address I was ushered into the garage to view the captive. My song shifted to "Muskrat Ramble." I moved the frightened creature from its box to my live trap and explained to the woman that it was a muskrat, brown, not gray like an opossum. As I left to take it to a pond out of town, I heard her mutter, "It's a possum."

One of my advanced biology students called on a weekend. "Miss Micken, I found this white flower, and want to know what it is."

"White flower?" My mind went through pages of white flowers in a wildflower book. "Can you describe it? How many petals?"

"Five, and it was a little plant."

I eliminated mustard and sunflower families and all shrubs.

"What do the leaves look like?"

"Leaves? I don't know. I have the flower on a little stem."

"Bring it to school Monday."

He delivered the badly wilted blossom as school opened. Unidentifiable. "Bring me the whole plant."

"I dunno if I can find it again. We were hiking up in the mountains."

End of visualizations of wildflower books. Identification unknown.

The junior high Home Ec. teacher called. "Lori, could you come and identify these worms we found in one of the sinks? I don't want to touch them until I know what they are."

"What do they look like?"

"White, round, about an inch long, skinny."

"I'll come over next period." In an hour I grabbed a binocular microscope, an invertebrate zoology book, tweezers, and a vial of alcohol, and drove the few blocks to the junior high.

I peered into the sink drain. Nothing moved. "They're not worms." I tweezered up a couple and put them on a glass slide under the microscope. "Ah hah! Plant roots, You're safe." I went back to my school and work.

Another call came, this time from the Park Clinic. "Dr. Basket would like to talk to you."

I'd not been to see him for ages so a sort of dread hit me.

"Lori, I have a big orb spinning spider on the sliding glass door here at my office. I don't like spiders, but I hate to kill this one. I can't use the door to the balcony. Could you come and get it?"

"Of course, doctor, I'll be right over." I captured it in a glass jar and took it home to adorn the house. Nice addition.

One fall, I called Bud Miles, a neighbor down the road a mile, to seek permission to grouse hunt on his ranch.

"Nope, I'm not allowing any hunters in this year."

A few days later, Bud called me. "Lori, a guy traps coyotes up here, and there's a badger in one of his traps. I don't want it killed. They eat gophers. Do you have something to put it to sleep so we can release it?"

I envisioned a very angry, hurting badger with its long claws and array of sharp teeth. "Yes, I have a bottle of chloroform I keep on hand to put down crippled chickens or lambs or whatever. A sick cat showed up here once. I got him cornered in the dog house and put him to sleep to take to the vet. My technique worked on him, so it ought to work on the badger.

"I'll be right down." I grabbed the chloroform, tied a rag to the end of a lathe, and was off.

Bud drove us into the upper ranch to the badger. It had torn up the ground some. It snarled and lunged at us. I soaked the rag with chloroform, and we backed it up as far as the trap chain would allow. Of course, it fought the stick and rag when I put it under that beautiful long black and white nose, but soon succumbed and sank to its side. I was fearful of overdosing, so took the rag away. Bud opened the trap, and we inspected its paw. It was swollen, but there was no blood, and it still looked okay. In a minute or so the badger came to, shook its paw, and limped off. One baleful look over its shoulder at us should have shriveled our souls. Mine soared at our good deed.

On the drive back to the ranch, Bud said, "I guess if you still want to grouse hunt you can, but stay west of the creek."

I seemed to be a repository for unwanted pets that people couldn't give away. Mungo, a ferret; Mergatrude, a small boa constrictor who grew to be six feet long and weigh 26 pounds; and a big green iguana, all came to the biology room in their donated cages. Gerbils, rats, and hamsters were also re-homed to me.

I would give students passes from study hall to take the animals out on the lawn in nice weather or to play with them and feed them in the lab in inclement weather. It was good for the animals and the kids.

I did refuse a monkey, complete with huge cage. Even I had limits.

My most incredible call came on a weekend from the mother of two of my students. "Miss Micken, we just moved into town from the ranch last week. I found a bunch of stuff way under the basement stairs. One thing is a quart jar with a human embryo in it. Can you come and get it out of here?

I thought, "Human embryo? No. Maybe a monkey or a puppy, kitten or lamb. Embryos are tiny, much alike in early stages, but a quart jar?" I drove into town after lunch. She met me at the door with a paper sack in hand.

"Here, please, take it."

"Let's take a look at it."

"I have. I want it out of here."

I opened the sack, took out the jar, and nearly dropped it. It was definitely a human fetus, about five months old, in a preservative. There were obvious bruise marks across his back and on the arm and leg on one side. Had he been aborted? The mother killed in a car wreck? What could've caused the bruises? And why the hell had he been interred in a preservative and placed far under the stairs, not properly buried? And why had he been left there when they moved?

I took him to school and put him in a back cupboard in the science teachers' workroom. I pondered what to do with him. The woman didn't want her name involved if I went to the authorities. This was in the 1960s, pre-DNA testing, and apparently, pre-my-good-sense.

I kept him for several years, showing him in the embryology unit in advance biology. The wonder of eyelids, finger, and toenails on perfectly formed digits, everything about him, including his sex were marveled over.

My housemate, Linda, a Catholic, eventually convinced me we should bury him. So, on a sunny summer day, we drove up into the mountains above Ennis and buried him—freeing him from the jar and alcohol. Pax vobiscum. The mystery remains. Who, when, why, how?

I'm long retired. No longer do I get amazing calls to identify organisms, or take care of animals. I totally enjoyed being Miss Biology for the town.

A MOUSE OF A DIFFERENT COLOR

In the spring of 1978, I applied for and received an all expense trip for a high school biology teachers' workshop in Denver. All of the sessions were interesting, but the one on mouse genetics appealed to me the most. Several genetically pure races on exhibit fascinated me. We could take some mice back to our classrooms. I selected four varieties: black, a reddish-brown, a tan pinto, and a palomino with a white diamond on its head. The bald race, the ones with the nerve disorder that had the poor things turning in circles much of their lives, and genetically obese mice didn't appeal to me.

Companion animals on airplanes had not been invented yet, but no one raised an eyebrow at my carry-on of two, foot-long cages with mice in them.

The next day and I showed my colorful mice to the biology classes. The intrigued students had many questions.

I had other cages at school and did some breeding over the summer to give ample specimens for advanced biology the next school year.

Their assignment for the school year was to endeavor to transfer a trait to another race, such as produce a black pinto or a diamond on a brown mouse, and to determine if they bred true. The partners conferred and wrote up their ideas, how to obtain them, and the genetics of their experiment. Notes were to be taken through the school year.

Two girls said they wanted to selectively breed for short tails as they noticed one mouse with a slightly shorter blunt tail. I said only genes for color could be dealt with. Besides, I doubted a gene for short tales existed. I would make a poor mother, for I gave in to their request.

The geneticists took a few minutes of class twice a week to take notes, clean, feed. and water their charges.

The two tailophyts took reports and mice from the other six pair of students on any mice with shorter or blunter tails. By the end of May, nine months of breeding, they miraculously had mice with tails like hamsters. My student lab assistants were unhappy with this experiment, as they cleaned and kept up the purebred and extra mouse cages, and it was too difficult to pick up the short-tailed mice. The ever-growing boa constrictor, Mergatrude, took any excess mice.

Come the end of school, the mousecapades had done well. Only the production of black mice with a white diamond (supposedly a dominant trait) had failed.

Rather than send my precious purebred lines home with students for the summer, I decided again to keep the mice. However, a trip back east, hiking Glacier National Park, and the care of livestock and garden looked like a full summer. When cleaning cages in the barn, one quick mouse escaped into the haystack. Perhaps I wasn't the best one to keep them. Friend Bette Lowery volunteered her mother on their ranch near Roundup to care for my fancy rodents for the rest of the summer.

Alice loves all animals and was delighted to take them. I drove to the ranch with two sacks of sawdust for bedding, feed, a cage of four males, one of four females, and two spare cages.

"For Pete's sake, don't mix the sexes. I don't want any more mice and have to keep the pure lines for next year's advanced biology lab."

"Oh, yeah, it'll be easy and fun, and I like the little devils."

A week before school started, I drove to Roundup to get my critters. Alice called "Come on in," when I knocked.

My heart sank when I went in the house. There on the shelf in the entry hall, sat four very empty cages. Had they all died? or worse, escaped? I called to Alice.

"Come in, come on in," she motioned me to the kitchen. "Looky here, ain't this something?" She pointed to two large garbage cans. They were alive with mice, black mice, every shade of brown mice, pinto mice of every hue, and white diamonds on a variety of mouse heads. Generations of happy mice.

I stared. "What happened?"

"Well, the second time I cleaned them, I got mixed up and accidentally put two of the females with the males. It took a lot of time to clean those little cages, so I brought in the garbage cans for them."

I couldn't take my eyes off the legions of mice. "How many are there?"

"I count them each time I clean them—53 now. They are so cute. See, I put an exercise wheel in for them, and give special treats like nuts and seeds and fruit, too. Ran out of your feed and sawdust, so they've had oats and cattle cubes, and hay for the bedding."

"They look healthy, Alice. You've done a wonderful job taking care of them." The rest of my thoughts couldn't be said. There would be no more genetics now. All I could do was laugh and think of the happy mice.

"How you going to get them home?"

"I'll put some in my cages. The garbage cans are too tippy to take in the car."

"Got just the thing, an old cooler chest and lots of screening to make a cover for it."

So, they were packed and taken to the school. I sorted sexes into separate cages. Mergatrude would be the happiest snake in the county.

P. S. Later that year, when checking the basement traps at home, I found a dead house mouse with a perfect white diamond on its forehead. If only it hadn't been killed, I'd have had the fanciest wild mouse ever.

Lodgepole pine forest and beargrass flowers

CAN'T SEE THE FOREST FOR THE TREES

I'm in love with forests. All the shades of green, the way they talk in the wind, swaying in arcs large or small depending on wind speed, the creaking of one fallen against another, the smells of pine resin and flowers, the bird songs, insects buzzing, and squirrels chirring. It is a miracle of ongoing life.

We name the forests for their major trees: the redwood forest, the spruce-fir forest, the loblolly pine woods (I love that musical name), and the birch-hickory forest. All are defined by the trees.

A forest is composed of the tallest canopy trees, an understory of tall brush and saplings, a shrub layer, an herb layer, and the floor. The two tallest layers are the major trees that cover the area. The rest are icing on the layer cake.

In western Montana in the early 1900s, immense fires destroyed miles of trees. The new forest that grew from the ashes was largely lodgepole pine, with some of the 200 or 300-year-old giant Tamarack's and firs that survived the blaze. Now, over 100 years after the conflagration, the lodge poles have aged and are dying. An understory of spruce, fir, and tamarack are growing in to replace the pines and form the climax forest—the final stage in succession.

There is more diversity in the shrub layer plants. Roses, willows, buffalo berries, huckleberries, honeysuckle and more, all crowd for space, sun, water, and nutrients. Below these are the herbs, such as bear grass, lupine, violets, orchids, asters, and many more. On the ground are fallen leaves, mosses, bark chips, twigs covered in black lichen, cones, and other tiny bits of beauty, such as colorful rock chips from the mountains to the east. There is a constant rain of debris from the layers above and a constant breakdown of complex materials into nutrients for the higher layers.

I picked up one rectangular piece of bark. The bark surface was the usual textured, mottled shades of gray. What used to be the inside against the cambian layer of the tree was a work of art, reminiscent of sand paintings. A wavy russet band made three hills. Above that, peach and rose-colored bands looked like clouds. A black line separated some light gray that looked like sky. This gorgeous little abstract could be framed as a miniature landscape.

The forest is more than trees. There is more beauty than the flowers, leaves, cones, and hundreds of thousands of jigsaw pieces that compose it. Little is known of all the relationships. It's been found that the plants, from fungi on up to the trees, "talk" to each other chemically, feed each other, perhaps warn each other of danger from insects and other predators.

Living things are far more complex in their communities than we ever dreamed, as complex as our own communities. I only hope our discoveries outrace the destruction we wreck upon them and ourselves, and that we will always have them to feed our souls.

FIRE SEASON

We come to the lake in the heavy August heat to be in the sweet, cool breeze across the water, with the smell of evergreens heavy in the air.

But today, August 2, 2015, the air isn't sweet. It's tainted with forest fire smoke from the northeast. The gray mountains are nearly hidden in it; only the treed area shows as black, irregular blobs. Across the lake it looks clear. Down lake I can see the haze in the trees. I can smell faint whiffs of burning forest.

Fire danger is "very high," down from "extreme" because of last week's nearly three-quarter inch of rain. There have been no lightning storms, so some irresponsible idiot left a campfire, or dropped a cigarette, or made sparks dragging the chain off the camper or trailer connection.

In years past, gigantic blazes have been started innocently enough. Once near Red Lodge a motorcyclist skidded and fell with his cycle. The hot engine ignited grass by the road, and a fire was off and running. North of Yellowstone Park, a shod horse made sparks on the rocks and fire came from it. Near Bozeman, a combine harvesting wheat heated its engine parts enough to cause combustion in the field, and another fire was running.

When nature starts the fires, it somehow doesn't seem as bad. Her lightning sparks create so much damage and kill many mammals, insects, reptiles, and amphibians that die horribly. For the individual, it is catastrophic, but for the general health of the forest, beneficial.

We drove north of the lake to find the source of this smoke and discovered the fire was within sight of the highway ten miles later, blazing up a mountain on the Swan Range. By now it was nearing the tree line and sheer cliffs, so unless an unfavorable wind arose, it would burn itself out. Firefighters were working to keep it contained to that drainage. A few years before, a controlled burn had been set to clear deadfall and undergrowth from a nearby drainage. It escaped a proposed burn area and turned into a wildfire. Both fires had the same effects.

On July 30, 2017, I drove to the cabin planning on spending a week there. At Seeley Lake I noticed a thin, smoke pillar to the north. A store clerk informed me it only covered about 60 acres and had started with a lightning strike. The next day, Monday, it had grown to over 1,000 acres, and we were getting some smoke at Pierce Lake. Tuesday over 2,000 acres were burning, and visibility was less than 100 yards. Such smoke makes my bronchitis far worse, so I drove back to my house near Livingston. Three fourths of the town of Seeley Lake had to be evacuated, as the flames came to within one and a half miles of town. Hot weather and dryness heightened firefighting problems, as did the rough terrain. The trees had only 15% moisture, as dry as kiln-dried lumber. The fire continued to grow, and in the end, it consumed over 160,000 acres, or 250 square miles—nearly ¼ the area of Rhode Island. Fires in the entire state burned an area equivalent to the size of New Jersey plus 500 square miles.

There are no statistics on how many squirrels and chickadees, orchids and roses, butterflies and beetles or other small creatures died in those miles of fire. I grieve as much for them as for the trees. The species will return; the individual is lost forever.

CORGI DOG

Dwarf dog, dog of the fairies—the dogs' shoulder markings are from the harnesses the fairies used when riding them—herd dogs, dogs of the Queen, Pembroke Welch Corgis. I'd seen them at the dog shows. I had to have one. They are so cocky, so frisky. The perked ears, and cute butts made good selling points, too.

Research led me to the Clarkin Kennels in central Idaho. Yes, they had a month-old litter of eight. Linda and I arranged a time to drive there, a 450-mile trip one way. I wanted a red female, like Queen Elizabeth's. There were two in the litter.

At Clarkin's, we sat on the floor of their basement pen and watched the chubby pups play. A little tricolor female kept coming over to me, trying to climb onto my leg. She was the runt of the litter, two-thirds the size of the others.

Kathy suggested we take the pups out in the yard to watch them play in a different environment. The same little tricolor came to me rather than playing with her siblings. She untied my shoes, crawled on my lap, and clearly said, "You are my human." We were in love. I paid $100 to hold her for five more weeks. We drove back in June for Clarkin's Kiera Spring Song, and paid the remaining $250.

I named her Kiera. Herding instincts showed immediately, though the chickens and ducks weren't impressed with this stubby pooch and backed her off a few times.

Every morning in summer, we took the sheep up the road to a pasture. Kiera instinctively knew her job was to keep the flock bunched together. If any strayed into the borrow pit, she immediately herded them back by barking and nipping at their heels. They minded better than the poultry. In the evening, we brought them back to the barn and corrals.

Kiera's adult weight topped at only 20 pounds, too small, I feared to use her to work the cows, but twice I needed help. Her yap and nip technique worked just as well on them. By mid-June the pasture grass grew to over her head. She had to jump up to see where the cattle were, then run toward them. She repeated this until she had caught up and could herd properly.

I wanted to show her in confirmation classes at the dog show, but she was too small and not up to their standards on other counts. So, I had her spayed. Unfortunately, this late spaying created problems with Linda's Yorkie, Skeeter. The two little dogs had gotten along fine before spaying. When I was alone with them, everything remained peaceful, but when Linda came home, Skeeter had to keep Kiera away from her. This possessiveness led to several bloody battles. Some of the blood mine, as Kiera bit me deeply on the hand when I tried to separate them in one battle.

Unfortunately, the friction never ceased until they were old dogs.

The dogs enjoyed going to the cabin as much as we did. Arriving at the cabin, Kiera would bolt out the open pickup door and either run up the driveway to the road, or race down the trail and north to Dave's, two tenths of a mile away. The first couple times I didn't realize where she had gone and worried until Dave showed up with her. After that, I'd go after her, sometimes meeting Dave returning her. Obviously, she was greatly enamored with him, but remained with me the rest of the time. Dave stopped by mornings on his walk around the lake with his golden retriever. This was cause for great jubilation on Kiera's part. Rosie didn't mind sharing him with the small admirer.

Loud noises terrified Kiera. Whether guns, thunder, or fireworks, she came to be held and hid her face in my arms. Therefore, she didn't hunt with me. But she was an ardent fisher dog.

She wasn't too keen on going out in the boat, but when I landed a fish, she was on it immediately with intent to eat rather than just kill. The same was true when stream fishing. That is my favorite means of catching dinner. The fish were generally too small to bother with a net, so I would just flip them up on shore. She would sometimes get to the fish before I did. Mostly the fish only had a couple of tooth marks if I was quick enough.

Kiera seemed to like to wade, but not swim. The exception came if I waded across the stream and stayed away from her for very long. Then she would brave the chilly waters and cross to me, often getting pushed downstream. She dried quickly by rolling on the stream bank plants, and lying on the warm, pebble beaches. Of course, I carried her back.

Fishing the Gallatin River one hot summer day, I caught a nice rainbow. Kiera ran into the shallows for it and started yelping. Fish disappeared into the pool and I had a terrified corgi on the line. The hook had come free and lodged in her lip. Fortunately, friend Bette grabbed her as she fled downstream. It took both of us to get the hook out by clipping off the barb and turning the hook part of it out of her lip. The incident didn't deter her in "helping" land future catches.

I always gave her the heart, liver and, kidneys for her work. The rest of the innards and heads went to the crayfish at the lake.

She was smart, and had a dozen tricks, among them, praying. She put her paws on a chair and dropped her head between them long enough for a quick sentence of the Lord's Prayer.

When visiting my old high school friend, Alice, in Spokane, Kiera came with. After dinner the first night, Alice started upstairs with the kids to put them to bed. I asked if my dog could join them in prayer. The kids thought this would be wonderful. They knelt with their folded hands on the bed and spoke their prayers, joined by Kiera between them. Alice asked them if they liked that. Anita said, "Oh, it was nice, but she didn't SAY anything."

Obviously, we needed to add on a new dimension to the trick.

Her vet bills were never more than shots and an annual checkup. She started sort of fading away, growing weaker, slower, and less and less exuberant. Her eyesight and hearing started fading. Eventually we had to part.

Our love affair had lasted over 15 years.

Scotch Highland bull with Hickory behind him

HOW TO AVOID HIGH TAXES

The second year at our country house, the tax bill increased 900%. Some astute assessor had switched agriculture classification to residential—all 20 acres! We paid the taxes under official protest and started battling the county. After a year, they did switch the residential area to our one-acre homestead lot, but they were checking all the legal aspects. To be classified as agricultural, one had to take in $1500 a year in agricultural products: hay, cattle, eggs, etc. This did not have to be profit just income.

We cut more than enough hay on the place for our three horses. Horses were considered hobby animals, not livestock, by the taxman. So, we had hobbyhorses. What to do?

We would buy cattle—a decision that ultimately led to a long line of expenses for feed, immunization, vet bills, building a corral, and a barn. And ultimately a longer list of hard, physical labor.

We bought two Hereford heifers from Milt Schaplo, a neighbor when I lived south of Bozeman. We had no bull, so we hired the vet to A.I. (artificially inseminate) them.

Shots to start ovulation increased that expense. One heifer didn't "take" (become pregnant), so the next fall, we sold her along with Cynthia's calf. Cattle are herd animals, so we bought two more Hereford heifers and had them A.I.ed. All three took. We kept the heifers for seed and sold the steer—another expense, to have the baby bull castrated.

Soon we had, by this reasoning—inductive, deductive, dumb-ductive—enough income to beat the taxes and become agricultural.

Linda knew how to knit and wanted to learn to spin wool and weave. Ranchers have put their kids through college with sheep flocks' earnings. What better way to make money? Planting in the garden would have done just as well. She bought two old ewes, a Suffolk and a Hampshire.

Cattle and horse fences do not keep sheep in, so we had to buy and put up sheep fence, saving a lot by doing it ourselves.

A neighbor down the road, Peggy Strong, raised Romney sheep, a good wool breed that the other two were not. She spun her wool and did weaving. Linda almost levitated when she saw Peggy's loom with some cloth partially done.

She bought a Romney ewe from her immediately. As a surprise for her birthday, I bought another a few days later.

Bill Strong, Peg's husband, delivered it, but the sheep escaped when unloading her into the corral. We chased that wild beast all over the field. Her instincts cut in, and she headed uphill to some rock outcrops and stood watching us toil up to her. Nimble as a Chamois in the Caucasus, she evaded us. We needed several sheepdogs or a platoon of marathon runners, but the sheep tired after an hour, and Bill managed to tackle her, once more proving the superiority of humans over lower animals.

Linda came home shortly after the capture, and I presented her with that *^#@±! surprise birthday ewe.

She borrowed a Suffolk ram from a friend in Stevensville, south of Missoula. Kathy warned us never to turn our backs on him and to always keep giving him the "I'm your boss" stare. He had butted her father and knocked him down once. I wasn't afraid, but leery. One evening when filling the water tank, Ram and I were eyeing up each other. I glanced down to see how close to full the tank was, and he hit me, knocking me back into some steel posts that leaned in the corner between the barn and corral. When I struggled to my feet, I grabbed a piece of corral pole and went after him, chasing him all over the corral and hitting him. He didn't come near me again.

Kathy drove over in a couple days to take him home. My back shoulder and hip were sore for days. Ram had done his job, though, and we had baby lambs in April.

Next, we purchased the 22-acre parcel of land across the road for more grazing for our growing flock and herd. This action was precipitated when a young couple with three kids and two dogs came to look at it. The man managed to get his station wagon stuck in the mud up the hill and walked down to see if I would pull them out with my Scout. I told him I couldn't, very sorry, and offered to call a wrecker for him. I didn't invite him into the house or offer a ride back to his vehicle. That was not nice, but I figured by the time they got out of there, plus the unforeseen expense of a wrecker, they would be cured of this place in the country.

Neither they nor anyone else came to look at it.

In a few days we had arranged with Mr. Stafford to buy Lot 11. We had no down payment, but he waved that, as the land was not selling very fast. He set up monthly payments with the same arrangement of having a balloon payment in 10 years. We were land rich with 42.7 acres, and there would be no kids or another house in the area.

We were also in debt up to our chins. More acreage meant more taxes, but more land helped us keep being classed as a ranch.

Our follies continued.

Scotch Highland cattle are wonderful shaggy creatures, smaller than our Herefords and Angus, but gentle in spite of their huge threatening horns. When buying electric sheep fence from Charles Howell up Springhill on the west side of the Bridger Mountains, we admired his "Scotty's."

He had an old cow that had been his mother's pet. He thought she had been bred, but she was 20 years old. She had mastitis, only had half a milk bag, and might not produce milk if she did calve out. Of course, I bought her.

Come spring she presented us with a tiny, woolly baby that looked more bear than bovine. Hickory had no milk, but we did. I had purchased a nursing bottle and a sack of milk replacer, including the essential colostrum. Unfortunately, the bundle of fur was a laddie, not a lassie.

Hickory had dropped him at the far northeast corner of the pasture, below a saddle in the hill. We took turns carrying him the quarter mile back to the barn, Hickory nearly nosing us and bellowing all the way. This was very exciting, as her horns had grown out to the side, up, and then forward, spanning 42 inches from tip to tip.

Laddie took to the milk bottle readily. In a short time, he learned to come when I called, Mama trailing behind. No matter the weather, I fed him every four hours for two weeks, then every six hours, then every eight.

One early morning, I felt I was in Scotland. A heavy fog covered our place, and out of the misty moor Laddie came bawling and running as fast as his furry legs would carry him. Then Hickory lumbered into view through the fog. She took excellent care of him, even allowing him to try nursing.

We borrowed Mr. Howell's Highland bull that spring. He was gentle as a puppy, a fortunate attribute. His horns, too, were impressive. The males' horns grow out and forward in a single wide curve.

One day I noticed that he had a squinty, runny eye. When he bedded down to chew his cud, I walked over to him, sweet-talking all the way, for a closer look. Indeed, it was bad. In what I feared might be my last act on earth, I reached over his right horn and lifted the upper eyelid. I saw a piece of plant material near the corner of his eye and took it out. Miraculously, he continued to lie perfectly still. The culprit was one piece of burdock seed. With the irritation gone and some ointment, the eye returned to normal in a couple of days, as did my heartbeat and shaking.

Back to taxes. With the sale of calves, lambs, and wool, we were now taking in over $1500 a year. However, expenditures doubled or tripled that of the income, and we spent too many hours caring for our critters, doing the hard, physical labor of fence building and handling hay bales. All this while teaching school.

But, by darn, we had beaten the assessor and were taxed as agricultural from then on.

Sasha

GREAT PYRENEES

In Cut Bank in the late 1940s, on most days, a giant white dog came by our house heading for downtown. He ignored other dogs that ran out to bark at him, neither looking at them nor veering from his route. I found out he visited various stores for treats on a regular basis. He was docile, aloof, and aristocratic, obviously of royalty, seeming to think every other dog or animal beneath his attention. I decided someday I would own one of these incredible Great Pyrenees.

It took over 25 years, but when living south of Bozeman, a neighbor had a litter of Great Pyrenees. I bought Baron Huguenot de' Mystic when two months old. Hug didn't play silly games with balls or toys. He'd sit on the patio, looking into the aspen woods, obviously thinking serious, big-dog thoughts on what to be when grown up.

September came and I went back to teaching, so he had to be alone much of the day. I fixed him a pig wire pen attached to pines in the groove by the house. That life didn't suit him, and he started escaping. Of course, when I was home we'd go walking or he'd follow me on horseback. I tried tying him one day, but Hug was gone when I returned from a short trip to town. Big, strong, carnassial teeth had neatly sliced the rope. I spent the evening calling, and went out searching at first light on my horse, Warlock. The snow lay in drifts two feet deep. Finally my guilt-ridden calls were answered with frantic barking. The rope had hung up, and he packed snow down to mud around the tree he'd hung up on. I cried with relief, untangled him, and we went home.

Keeping a huge dog alone in the house all day would be impossible, as he stayed in all night. Neighbors with two little kids and a fenced yard said they would take him. Shortly after coming in their house the first time, he anointed their Christmas tree and some presents, so he was returned to me that same day.

Cousin Darrell in Missoula found a home for him up there: folks with a huge chain-link fenced yard. I left my dream dog with many tears and gloomy feelings of inadequacy and angst.

In 1978, Linda Stewart and I bought land 10 miles west of Livingston, the perfect place for a big dog. Pyrenees leapt to mind. Fortune struck as a newspaper ad, "Older great Pyrenees female for sale." I called the number immediately. These folks had rescued her from a small chain-link kennel, deep in mud and feces, but decided such a big dog was not for them. Oddly enough they had her registration papers. She originated in the famous Castellon kennel back east. Of course, we took her.

We discovered she had a phobia about mud and would not go near it. She would go off by herself toward the creek and make a nest in the grasses above any chance of getting in the water. When found, she'd willingly come home with us, but she desperately needed the freedom to be her own Pyrenees.

Tasha, was outside overnight at 48° below zero. Of course, the prediction wasn't for that low, or we'd have had her in the house. The next morning, we found her curled up in the hay shed in an "L" of bales, toasty warm.

Dogs need dog company, or so we reasoned before Tasha died. When another ad showed up in the paper for a half Pyrenees, half-wolfhound puppy, we bought her, but that's another story.

By now, we had joined the Great Pyrenees Club of America and located a puppy in Colorado. She was five months old, older than we wanted, but we had her flown up to us. Ripples Frosted Lady (Tassy) and Tawny got along beautifully. We also had our "indoor" little dogs, a Yorkshire terrier and a dachshund. Life was good.

A Pyrenees club member in California called us. She, a lawyer, her husband, two children, and two Pyrenees had recently moved there from Washington D.C. The children and dogs were used to human companionship all day in the form of a nanny. The children, now in school, no longer needed a nanny. The female Pyr proceeded to tear the house apart because of separation anxiety. She tore down the drapes, chewed on the couch, and ripped out a screen. If left in the yard she dug her way under the fence, escaping and causing great stress. Would we take the dog?

We explained that we had four dogs and that this Pyr sounded like more than a handful. After much tearful pleading, we told her we would consider it and call back tomorrow. "I already have her flight arranged for tomorrow. She'll be coming into the Bozeman airport about 4 o'clock." We begged her not to do that, but she said it was already done. I guess that's what makes a good lawyer.

Sasha weighed 115 pounds. She had the Karolaska fluffy show coat, so looked even bigger. We now owned over 400 pounds of dog.

Our kennel is chain-link and has a cement floor. Sasha started working on pushing out some of the chain-link at the bottom and finally succeeded in escaping with her nose and top of her head bloodied. She got out of the yard by going to a corner, "walking" up the two sides. and lunging over. Eventually she settled down and decided this would be home.

She had a thunderous bark, fitting more for a mastiff than a lovely white lady. I can still see and hear her advancing down the deck, just her tail and top of her head showing over the windowsill, roaring an alert to whatever she perceived as an invasion.

In the winter when there was a full moon or close to it, we would often walk the dogs at night. The lighting then is glorious, like predawn or dusk, with moonlight reflected everywhere. When we got to the brush at the creek, just at the edge of the circle of light from the yard light, Sasha stopped and refused to be led on. It took us a few minutes to realize she was afraid of the dark. She was a city dog from both sides of the continent, and apparently had never been out at night outside the city lights. She soon got over that fear.

Pyrenees do not do well in obedience training. Their reaction times are slow, and they are too independent by nature. Nonetheless, we decided to work with Tassy and Sasha, and go to the Great Pyrenees national specialty in Olympia, Washington. We also entered them as a pair in obedience. This means having both dogs on your left side with the dogs executing all the commands: heal, trot, walk, sit, stay, and downs, in unison. We had them professionally washed and groomed. Sasha had to wear a bib to keep the magnificent pile of chest fur clean.

The first night, we stayed at the Orange Street Inn in Missoula, having arranged to have two large dogs in the room with us. About half an hour after checking in, we had a call from the office, requesting us to come to the lobby with our dogs. Fearing that we were being evicted, we slowly walked down. A clerk who had checked us in introduced us to the night shift women, everyone petting and hugging our giant dogs. "We just wanted the night crew to see your dogs. They are so impressive."

Thursday we drove to Olympia. Friday the opening parade of Pyrs to start the show had two hundred dogs and puppies parading around the hotel ballroom, carpeted with Astroturf for the event

Obedience work with Pyrs is almost comical, the dogs lumbering through the various orders, seemingly reluctantly. The "sit" command goes through the brain, down the spinal cord, into the back legs, which are slowly lowered to the sit position. Such slow motion is consistent with all commands. On the "down stay" one embarrassed woman's dog proceeded to crawl the 20 feet to her instead of waiting in place. I took first place in the pairs group, being the only one who actually finished all the parts of the routine. Both dogs took ribbons in the singles. It was a marvelous, ego-inflating experience.

Sasha finally found her true vocation. Linda bought a $900 bred Shetland ewe in South Dakota. Two days after the ewe's twins were born, she died. Linda decided to test Sasha's instincts, and brought the lambs to her in the yard. We could almost hear her say "my babies" when she received the two, five-pound lambs. Sasha bathed them, laid with them curled against her tummy between her legs, showed them around the yard, and did everything but feed them. After a month of tender care, we put them out with the other sheep. Sasha looked for them as the flock went to pasture and returned in the evening. The lambs didn't return the favor.

Kobi, our last Pyrenees, we purchased from a Montana breeder. She'd been sold to a sheep rancher, but Bonnie warned him that she probably wouldn't bond with the flock, as she was three months old. She kept leaving the sheep to return to the house. The rancher beat her, and returned her to the flock. When Bonnie drove to check on her, she found an emaciated, cowed dog, full of ticks and fleas, and with matted hair. She immediately loaded her in her car, returned the purchase price, and took her home to be nursed to health.

We had to wait over a month before getting her. It took a few weeks for her to get over her fearfulness, but always anyone in a cowboy hat, or carrying a shovel or other long-handled tool sent her into fearful barking and snarling, backing away in a crawl. My hatred for that rancher is unending.

Great Pyrenees' coat is gorgeous. There is an undercoat of fine fur, soft as any high-grade wool, and a three-inch long loose outer coat. One year, we decided to keep the combings from Sasha and Koby. After several months we had two huge black garbage bags of their fur. An acquaintance, Crystal, did the first ugly jobs of washing, carding, and spinning. Mrs. LeFevre, a dog club member, knit the rovings into two sweaters and two hats. They are luxurious. People guess them to be mohair or cashmere. The only problem with them is they are too hot to wear. I erred in wearing my sweater to teach. By the end of first period, I literally had sweat running and taught the rest of the day in the cotton turtleneck I'd worn under it. Even outside on a sub-zero day, no jacket is needed. Fur, designed for high-mountain sheep herding is soft and lustrous. No, the sweaters and hats don't smell "doggy."

An era ended when Kobi died. Giant dogs were getting harder to handle as they and we aged. It had been a grand run with incredible, beautiful dogs. I still miss having truly big dogs.

Bringing the Christmas tree home.
Lori with Tawny and Kobi, Great Pyrenees

USE THE SLED

If at all possible, I like to save trips, no matter the chore. I decide to take two straw bales from the stack to the barn at once. They are light enough to put on the calf sled, and it's all downhill. (A calf sled is made of very heavy plastic with about a four-inch rim on it to hold a baby calf while being moved.)

As the trail slips between the two garden fences, I catch an image in my mind's eye of acceleration down the steepest part, collision with the corral gate, or me smashed by either the bales or the sled. So, I stop to regroup. Unfortunately, the sled doesn't. One edge hits the fence, and several old laws of physics come to mind and into immediate play. The front of the sled stops. The rear continues in an arc of centrifugal force. Friction is totally lost; gravity pulls the sled down in a fit of propulsion somewhat faster than mine. I push on the hay shed with one hand to stop my momentum and swing up on the gate with the other arm.

The following day at the doctor's office, it's a bit hard to explain a pulled shoulder muscle from a sensible standpoint.

The next time I get lazy with the calf sled, I place two hay bales on it from the small stack by the garage. That makes a load of about 150 pounds, but again it's all downhill. This time I'm taking the hay from the driveway down through a gate into the pasture to the cattle feeder. The snow is knee-deep, but there is a sort of trail where I've gone down before. Remembering my shoulder, I'm careful to go at a creep and stop the sled before opening the long aluminum gate. It swings open, and I turn to pull on the sled. Nothing moves. So I give a big jerk and it moves, crashing into my lower right leg.

The leg remains painful for a couple of weeks and doesn't seem to be getting any better. At the doctor's office he takes an X-ray and finds the shinbone is cracked where the front edge of the sled hit it. After waiting two weeks, he says it would do no good to put on a cast, just let it heal and stay off it is much as possible.

Finally, I use the sled for its original purpose. Linda, my housemate, and I plan calving in April, but it can still snow, which it does this year. One of the cows had gone uphill into the aspens and dropped her baby in about a foot of snow. After finding her, we go back for the sled and return to the woods. Cynthia, the Hereford/Scotch Highland cow, is very protective and equipped with horns. We park the sled and go up to collect the baby, throwing down a pad of hay as enticement for mama. As I reach the calf, Linda circles uphill, and Cynthia feels her baby is trapped between us. Our aspens are small trees, mostly three to six inches in diameter. I manage to get behind a larger one as Cynthia charges. Fortunately, she hits the tree instead of me. I yell at Linda to get the hell out of there so the cow won't feel surrounded. Cynthia goes back to check her newborn, and I start sweet-talking her. She remembers she is gentle and lets me pick up her calf and take him to the sled. The calf is cold enough that he doesn't struggle. With both of us pulling the sled, Cynthia follows behind, and we're soon safely back at the barn with plenty of straw for the baby to lie in.

Most of the time the calf sled is used to haul hay from the stack below the barn to the sheep pasture or feeders. Our Irish wolfhound, Tawny, is pressed into service to do the hauling, one bale at a time. She has a real sled dog harness, special ordered, size extra large. She weighs 165 pounds and can pull a hay bale uphill into the sheep pasture in knee-deep snow as fast as we can walk. We toss flakes of hay off to the side for the sheep that follow along the trail we break. When the hay is delivered, we unhook Tawny, get in the sled, and race her back to the gate. She always wins.

I am still using the old orange sled; only now it is at my cabin to haul cooler chests, a suitcase, and other things down to the cabin from the car, then back when I'm ready to leave. There aren't as many adventures, as Tawny, the sheep, and cattle are gone. I don't have any injuries, either, but I long for my wolfhound and even miss the livestock, the snow, and cold.

The sled may appreciate semi-retirement, too.

WOLFHOUNDS

An Irish wolfhound is a sight to behold. I have been privileged to own two of "the dogs of Irish kings."

To tell the truth, Tawny, who Linda and I bought as a fluffy, white puppy, was half Great Pyrenees. Thinking she would look like a Pyr when grown, we answered the newspaper ad, and drove up toward Bridger Bowl ski area to get her. We met both mom and dad. The wolfhound father trotted along on top of a shoulder high snow bank, eyeing us as he might a leg of lamb. We had read that wolfhounds were gentle creatures, but he totally unnerved us. We followed the path to the barn to get the pup. I carried the 15-pound puppy, then eight weeks old, back to the car. Her daddy again followed along on the snow bank, totally intimidating us.

At that time in January, we had to snowshoe half a mile up to the house from the road. Carrying a wiggly 15-pound puppy was difficult, so I had her walk part way. She stuck with us, bounding through the snow. At home, we introduced her to the resident Yorky, Brier, and dachshund, Shatten. They were not impressed, but tolerant.

The people we bought her from warned us that she needed to eat a great deal in order to be healthy and grow properly. They recommended feeding her three times a day, which we did. We had purchased a baby playpen to confine her to the kitchen. This she quickly outgrew.

Indeed, she did eat! The rate at which she grew amazed us. We measured her shoulder height and weight once a week. I regret I didn't keep those figures. When she came, she could walk under a chair in the kitchen. That only lasted a couple of weeks, but walking under the kitchen table also became impossible for her. She quit growing when two years old. She then weighed in at 185 pounds, measured 32 inches tall at the shoulder, and seven feet from nose tip to tail tip. Her front paw covered the palm of my hand, roughly three inches in diameter. She would put her front legs over our shoulders so her head rose above ours. We did slim her down to 165 pounds when she finally finished her puppy growth. However, this was not the Great Pyrenees we had hoped for. She ended up with a wiry, light-tan wolfhound coat, complete with the proper ears and facial fixtures. Those wolfhound eyebrows could be worked separately or together and express everything from amazement to sorrow. To all appearances, we had a dog of Irish kings.

The yard is enclosed in a four-foot, chain-link fence. If she wanted out, she simply walked to the fence and would sort of flow over it. She didn't seem to jump, just stood or sat next to it, rose up on her hind legs and moved to the other side. She never went far, really quite a homebody. One of her favorite places to stay was on the deck on the east side of the house, where she could survey much of her kingdom. One day when looking south, her ears went up, she tore off the deck, over the fence, across the pasture, through the brush, and up on the next hill. We knew there was a badger family there, and often watched them through the binoculars. Tawny shortly returned at a trot. She came over the fence as easily as ever, only this time her jaws held a dead, nearly grown badger. She refused to give it up, so I went in the house and got a big milk bone that I traded her for the badger. I picked it up by the scruff and was amazed at its weight—about 10 pounds—and how easily she had carried it a quarter-mile or so. I returned it to its den, feeling terrible. The badgers moved out.

In nice weather, I would open the back of our Scout so she could lie in it and guard the driveway. We taught her that chickens, ducks, and geese were not prey animals. One day when I checked on her, she was lying on the tailgate with front paws crossed, watching a grouse family saunter up the lane. Apparently, she thought these were chickens and were to be left alone.

Wolfhounds are sight hounds. That is, they rely on vision rather than smell to locate prey. I didn't take her along when I hunted for deer on the ridges behind our house, as I felt she'd chase anything we saw. One day, Linda drove me to the top of the ridge so I could hunt down. When she returned to the house, she discovered Tawny had escaped the yard. About this time, I encountered my joyous wolf, running up the draw to meet me. I acted equally happy to see her.

"Meanwhile, back at the ranch," Linda again drove to the top of the ridge. She could not see either the dog or me and returned home. We all rendezvoused at the house about the same time. After that, I took Tawny along. She would go a short distance ahead, then step out to a vantage point to survey, usually the same spot I picked. We seldom got grouse or deer, but hunting became more pleasurable for me. Watching a fellow hunter scan with eyes and nose more than made up for no success.

I started taking her to Roundup, MT with me antelope hunting, but left her in the Scout while I walked. One morning I shot a buck, but he ran out of sight up a draw. I checked where he had stood and found quite a bit of blood. I ran back to the vehicle, released Tawny, showed her the blood trail, and she took off. I caught up to her, licking blood off the dead antelope. He did not run far, but I'd have had difficulty finding him in the high sage and junipers and around a bend in the draw. I didn't have a game sled with me or Tawny's harness, but she gave great dancing moral support on the drag back to the Scout.

We did have successful grouse hunts, and one time I had her drag a deer for me, using her harness. All I had to do was grab a leg occasionally to flip the deer off a sagebrush or shrub.

We had special ordered a sled dog harness. A phone call came to verify the sizes we'd sent, as it was so huge they didn't believe our figures. We used her to haul hay, too, and bring up feed when we were snowed in. She could pull 80 to 100 pounds uphill on the toboggan the half-mile from the car to the house through knee-deep snow faster than we could follow—on snowshoes. Fridays we would buy big sacks of dog food, chicken feed, and horse oats. Saturdays we would snowshoe out with Tawny and have her haul them home.

We belonged to Gallatin Dog Club, and decided to put her in obedience trials. It took six times to get her three "legs" for the lowest level of obedience. At one meet, she fell in love with a woman being one of the two "posts" the dogs had to do a figure 8 around. She was disqualified for leaning on her, or sitting in front of her, giving a paw to beg to be petted.

Tawny loved eating berries, chokecherries, hawthorn, serviceberries, and even rose hips. To get those, she would curl back her lips and gently remove the hip with her incisors, crunch it up, swallow, and go on to the next. Huckleberries at the cabin put her in paradise. She ate them as the bears do—taking an entire stem in her mouth and stripping it of fruit and leaves. The other dogs picked as we picked, berry by berry. Tawny made such a mess, we never followed her into a patch.

She developed anal gland problems to the point our vet, Connie Van Luchene, thought it best to remove them. A "cone" around her head the size to fit her would have been lethal to the rest of the household, so she made a contraption of six laths and straps along Tawny's sides to keep her from reaching back to lick and chew stitches. A couple days later, we drove up to the cabin. The next day, Tawny finally managed to turn enough to break the six laths and lick those itchy stitches. Fortunately, a neighbor up there, Dave Peterson, was a handyman. He had some oak flooring and reconstructed the contraption with that. He carefully rounded the ends and edges. The oak she could not break.

But all things, even good ones, must end. At nine years old, Tawny contracted bone cancer in her right front ankle. We had a good summer and fall, though. A last successful Hungarian partridge hunt, the last hike on the ridge top, a last rabbit chase, the last days on the deck in the sun. Our vet came to the house to "beam her up."

About two years later, we received a call from Wolfhounds Rescue in Glasgow, Montana. Would we be interested in a three-year-old Irish wolfhound in Helena, Montana? A young woman, as a gift for her mother, had brought the dog from Ireland. Both women worked, so the dog was alone all day. They were prompted to turn her over to Wolfhound Rescue the day she brought home a freshly killed fox.

Of course, we took her, and named her Shillelagh. Compared to Tawny, she was petite; gazelle-like legs, narrow head and muzzle, thin tail, and racy body. In fact, we thought she looked more like a Scottish deerhound. Her wiry, gray coat did include facial and muzzle furnishings that enabled her to have 100 facial expressions. Her nature could best be described as gentle. She didn't jump the fence, didn't chase anything, and never got over five feet from us on walks. Hunting didn't interest her, but she did play with the little dogs. She loved riding in our vehicles, sleeping on the deck with the barn cat, and effusively greeting company. She had a wonderful toothy grin.

By this time, we had a snow fence to keep the road clear much of the time, so Shillelagh didn't have to haul in goods from the car, but she did haul hay to the barn. She, too, loved being at the cabin but didn't eat huckleberries.

Unfortunately, she contracted bone cancer, too, and died at nine, every inch a king's dog.

Linda Stewart at entrance to tunnel on trail to Crypt Lake

CRYPT LAKE

I had hiked most of the trails on the east side of Glacier National Park, usually by myself. Crypt Lake in Waterton Park was not one I wanted to go on alone, as the Guide to Glacier called it "the most challenging of popular trails in Waterton/Glacier Park." I had kept moving it down my list until I had a hiking companion. Linda Stewart agreed to make the trip with me.

We drove from Livingston 230 miles to my cabin for an overnight, then on through Glacier Park, and north to Waterton Townsite in Canada. We had rented a motel room there for two nights.

A perfect day dawned for the hike. Even in the park, August can get hot, but this promised to be only moderately warm. To reach the trailhead, a boat trip across Waterton Lake and part way up the east side is necessary. The boat continues on several miles to the end of the lake in the U.S.

The boat left on time and deposited several others and us at a dock with an open shelter close to the water. One tricky part of the hike is to get back to the shelter and dock before the last boat comes down-lake to return to Waterton Townsite. Most of the group that came ashore was going to stay at the campground overnight to make a more leisurely trip. It is five miles to the campground and an additional half-mile to the lake.

A Blackfoot man was the only hiker I remember. Although these parks were within their ancestral territory, I've never seen another of the tribe or any Native American out hiking. He blazed up the trail, passing everyone. I wondered if one of his ancestors might have come up here for a vision quest.

The shorter branch of the trail climbed through a heavy evergreen forest, up two easy switchbacks, and across the mouth of Burnt Rock Canyon. Then we confronted a gut-busting 500-foot climb by way of 12 short switchbacks, stacked one above the other like ladder rungs. At the top, we looked down on all 12 switchbacks and watched our fellow hikers laboring up.

Shortly after that, we reached the small campground. We made a quick stop there to use the pit toilet and get out our lunches of granola bars and oranges to eat as we walked. Everyone else stayed in camp. The trail became a scratch, only 20 inches wide along the face of a limestone cliff. Ahead we could see Crypt Falls dropping over 600 feet into the canyon. Carefully creeping along the ledge, the falls didn't seem to be getting any closer because of our slow progress. The trail ended at the bottom of an eight-foot, vertical, metal ladder attached to a sheer rock wall.

At the top of the ladder, we turned right into the mouth of the tunnel we had read about in the guidebook. A natural tunnel through this spine of limestone had been enlarged by the park service. At best, it was only about three feet high so we had to remove our packs and shove them ahead of us. Crawling wouldn't work as we wore lederhosen (leather shorts), and bare knees on the rock would've been abrasive. Ambulating on all fours is hard enough in the open. In this tunnel, we had to be cautious not to scrape our backs on the rough rock ceiling. Shove pack ahead; right hand, left foot, left hand, right foot, shove pack, hand, foot, hand, foot, etc. for over 60 feet: a very slow passage spider-walking like that. At the other end, it was a relief to stand, stretch, and replace our packs.

A cable set on hefty iron posts helped us over a rough scramble that angled across more limestone chunks. We wondered what brave souls had drilled in the holders and put up the ladder and cable, and also who first found Crypt Lake. It seems unlikely the Blackfeet would have searched for the source of the waterfall. There is no way that anyone other than an expert rock climber could have gone up the box canyon and scaled the cliffs beside the waterfall. Coming this way would have been a near-death experience without the improvements. We put those discoverers in the same class as the early sailors who dared go out to find the edge of Earth when they believed it to be flat.

At the end of the cable, the trail gave us an easy hike to and across a terminal moraine. At the top, we finally saw Crypt Lake. There were only a few alpine trees and scattered herbs in its rocky bowl. We saw three hikers at the other end of the lake, which is in Montana.

We walked down to Crypt and put our hands in its frigid waters. There is no outlet stream. Water seeps through the rocks to leap over Crypt Falls. We decided not to walk around the small lake as time was catching up to us. Our boat had left Waterton Townsite at 9 o'clock. The last boat back there would leave the dock and shelter at 5:30, and it was now almost 3 o'clock with five and a half miles to go.

We reversed our harrowing trek. Hanging onto the cable going down was harder than the ascent had been. The crawl through the tunnel proved just as tough. Stepping off onto the ladder gave us pause. Looking down 600 feet into the canyon, there seemed to be nothing but air at the base. The ledge felt narrower on this return trip. A cable to hang onto would have been welcome here. Our fellow passengers were in camp, relaxing. Fortunately, we had seen no one else on the trail. There was no room for passing fellow hikers in that half-mile stretch of ledge, ladder, tunnel, and cable scramble.

Traversing the switchbacks was just as tough on legs as uphill, jolting at each step down. Hurrying is impossible on such a treacherous decline.

At last we reached the relatively easy trail through the woods. We had made good time. We came to the lake and were shocked to find no dock, no hiker shelter. I jerked the guidebook from my pack to check. No, no, no! We missed a sign on our rush for the boat and were on the old, longer trail along the lake. We panicked. The guide didn't say how much further this was, and we were nearing exhaustion.

If we missed the boat, we were stranded. There is no bridge across the outlet river of Waterton Lakes, miles to the north. No one would know we had missed the boat. (This was pre-cellphone era.) The Narrows between the two lakes would be impossible to swim across. There might be a chance of hailing a private boat and 99 chances there would not be one. So, we had two choices: catch the boat or spend the night in the very open shelter by the dock. We were edging on dread.

A night in the three-sided shelter with no food or blanket seemed ghastly. I thought of the old Scottish prayer, "From ghoulies and ghosties, and long-legged beasties, and things that go bump in the night, good Lord, deliver us." We feared there would be a lot of "beasties" and bumps in the night if we had to spend the night in that open lean-to by the lake. Cold would be another beasty.

Suddenly, spurs were figuratively set to us. The boat's warning toot of departure sounded. It seemed rather close, but we couldn't really tell. Adrenalin is wonderful. We started to dogtrot through another dip in the trail and around the bend of the bay. The boat was still at the dock. We screamed, "Wait, wait, wait!" The guy untying the lines looked up and waved. We'd made it.

Worn out, we sagged onto a bench in the boat, the first we'd sat to rest since 9:15 that morning. We felt like Crypt Lake nearly was our crypt, but we had done it. We hiked the most challenging trail in the parks, one listed by National Geographic as "one of the 20 most challenging hikes in the world." Elation hit us. After all the years of waiting, the hike was worth it. Instead of jumping up and down and yelling, all we could do was lean back on the hard bench, stretch out our legs, and grin.

Arrow-leaved Balsamroot in May. White flowers are chokecherry.

SPRING WILDFLOWERS

The first wildflowers appear in March like color in a gold miner's pan: a breathtaking pleasure, value beyond counting. I search for them as eagerly as any miner sought bonanza. The first ones are golden: wild carrots, an intense canary yellow; buttercups, of course butter yellow. Generally they get snowed on, frozen, and battered by vicious winds. Fortunately they are so low to the ground that they managed to survive. The spring beauties bloom next, their white petals with pink veins sprinkle like stars in the Milky Way across the greening grass where the snow had drifted deep all winter. More white flowers are Hood's Phlox, five-petaled plain Janes with greens that look like moss. All are in a hurry to be the first to soak up water and sunlight, to get on with the job of reproduction.

After a few days and yet another snowstorm, I cross my road into the ram pasture, seeking more species. After yellow, white, yellow, white I gasp when I find the magenta shooting stars, their five, slightly-twisted petals pulled back from a dark point, appearing to be a comet on a stalk. The thrill is like seeing the first skyrocket in a fireworks display. Nearby I find the orangey-yellow drooping flowers of yellow bells, white and lavender crocus, pale purple spikes of kitten tails and, in a rocky outcrop, the impossibly dark pink Mountain douglasii. Nosegays of yellow violets replace the fading buttercups. In the next weeks, dozens of species large and small come into bloom, spreading prism colors across the hills.

The first flowers die, dry, and disappear. By the end of May, sagebrush grasslands look mainly yellow with the cumbersomely named Arrowleafed Balsamroot. Many people call them spring sunflowers. Sprinkled in among them are purple larkspur, blue chiming bells, and lupine.

There are a few reds, such as scarlet paintbrush and oranges like scarlet globemallow. The entire spectrum of color can be found, even greenish flowers. My high school biology students loved the name Pale Bastard Toadflax. Grasses and sedges also bloom, though about all we notice are the seed heads they produce.

Dozens and dozens of species of flowers grow and manufacture their seeds through the summer. The show is almost over when sunflowers, goldenrods, purple gay feathers, white prairie asters, and lavender-colored smooth asters bloom. (The latter is another my students loved to play with the syllables to call them smooth-ass-ter.) In the fall there are stinky coastal tarweed, and tiny—flowered knotweed. Apparently, these flowers make the plant attractive as food. The sheep eat them like candy and I've seen squirrels and chipmunks seek them out to eat, but not until they bloom.

Nothing, however, is as appreciated as those first fragile, brave blossoms. They are as thrilling as a roller coaster ride. They show winter is indeed dying, and the warm weather and soft rains will come. They are harbingers of the hills turning green and the trees and bushes leafing out. They bring the message of days lengthening, darkness being driven away, and rainbows every day.

SUMMER, JUNE 21

I would stop the earth right here, half a step beyond summer's birth, a day without wind, temperatures in the 70s, and every green and young thing still growing rapidly, exploding with vigor.

Yesterday morning, I heard the first wren. Today a tiger swallowtail butterfly dazzled with his erratic flight plan over the garden, fusing with several flowers on the lilacs. At evening I found two Cecropia moths mating—a pairing of beautiful furry russet, white, and charcoal wings and bodies. Dozens of other butterflies and moths dart and dance in the early summer's sun or gentle evenings. The young grasshoppers are out, and just as unfortunately the half dozen species of flies that plague livestock and their owners.

Time is mine now, to spend or waste as I see fit. There is no schedule but day and night, and the time for each flower to bloom, set by sun's angle and hours of light. The scents of lilacs and roses in the yard and the chokecherry blooms along the creek make me stop and go giddy with their perfume. I can sit and let time run with the creek. Two more months of summer stretch ahead: time to write, to watch the dogs play, to work, to garden, to fish, and to think.

Venus rides low in the sky like an airship, guardian of spring and companion to summer constellations. The moon has a lower arc now, following the path the sun takes in winter.

It is so quiet, the tiny creek, still high from snowmelt, can be heard from a hundred feet away. It will start to slow and calm soon, but will still hold the magic of water running free.

Early spring flowers are nearly gone: pink and white trillium, buttercups, yellow bells, fuchsia shooting stars, and yellow glacier lilies. However, the later-blooming, scarlet Indian paintbrush, golden arnica, purple lupine, and orange mallow are just as beautiful. Even the grasses' tiny flowers, looked at through a hand lens, give beauty as well as promise of the future harvest.

Work, too, helps fill the senses. The bouquet of newly mown lawn floats in the air. It would be good to have a bottled scent of summer to strew about the snowbound house six months from now.

The Bible says, "For everything there is a season and a time for every matter under heaven." This is nearly the midpoint of the year. Autumn is lovely, but it is a dying season. Late life becomes grim. I would live my life out in a forever summer, and then go out like our exploding sunsets—colorful, silently, grandly, without pain or fear.

If there is a heaven, in no way can it exceed the summer season on Earth.

No, disturb me not. Here I shall stay: dreaming the time away and hoarding summer's heat and heady combinations that pique senses to new alertness. The year is half gone, my life mostly gone. I shall ponder that, and become one with summer's priceless treasures.

IN THE ASPEN WOODS

I have two aspen groves on my property. Each is a clone of one tree that grew there, probably hundreds of years ago. It sent out roots, and gradually put up new trees from those roots. Aspen are short-lived trees, individuals generally living only 50 to 60 years. However, the entire clone may live to be 80,000 years, the oldest living things on earth.

Spring arrives. First the trees' flowers bloom: long catkins like fuzzy caterpillars. Then, bundles of leaf buds that look like fir needles arrive. These "needles" unfurl to the nearly round young leaves that are rust colored. Soon the grove is covered with apple green leaves. Gradually they darken to their summer jade. Walking in among these trees when even a light breeze is blowing, I hear rustling, whispering, and sighing, as though from spirits.

The air's odor is an ethereal mix of water, moist soil, a vague whiff of turpentine, and an intoxicating scent from new growth.

Young aspen bark is beautiful—smooth, unblemished. I love the feel of the powdery covering on it. It comes off with just a quick rub and feels like talc.

Aspens don't grow straight. I found two young ones twisting about each other in a frozen dance, one with a full 360° curl. Others develop bends as they rise toward the sun. A great many of the trees die young, broken by heavy, wet snows, winds, or animals. Sometimes, buck deer, cleaning velvet from their antlers, strip their bark.

There are some new, two-inch tall baby trees starting this spring, rising as suckers off the "mother" trees' roots. In a wet year, new trees venture out further from the rest. They may be doomed, being unfortunate enough to grow where it becomes too dry for several years.

Twenty-five years ago, while eating dinner, the kitchen filled with blinding light and simultaneous ear-splitting thunder—a thunderbolt to make me cringe. The next day I walked up the hill and located the shattered aspen that the lightning had struck. I could see no reason it was targeted. It stood at the edge of the grove, certainly not the tallest, and only about three inches in diameter. Another of nature's caprices.

They do not age gracefully. Where twigs break off, black areas remain, giving each tree a special character. Any wound also causes black spots. As they age, the lower bark becomes grooved and dark chocolate-colored for a few feet up. The dead, derelict old trees make good homes for cavity-nesting birds that can easily chisel into their soft wood. When they die, the bark sloughs off gradually, showing a silvery gray wood. Heavy bark at the bottom peels in chunks. I found these make excellent tinder, as layers can be taken off and strings of the black under-bark torn into shreds.

Aspens have many predators. The most noticeable are the poplar borer beetles, who drill into the tree to lay their eggs. The tree responds with a drool of orange-gold sap that runs down the trunk and hardens. Hairy woodpeckers cut roughly rectangular holes through the bark into the heartwood, searching for grubs. Sapsuckers drill a line of holes and dine on the sap. I tasted a tiny amount of this that was still liquid. I would not make a good woodpecker. It was more bitter than alkali and difficult to wash out of my mouth.

I find where caterpillars have chewed out pieces of the leaves. Brittle black spots from fungi mar them, too. There are aphids sucking the juice from leaves making them curl and die, Leaf miners, tunneling between the cell layers, leave translucent paths winding about in the leaf.

Aspens' greatest beauty is in autumn. The leaves turn a brilliant yellow. With rare weather conditions they become saffron, orange, or red. Days must be very warm, and nights close to, but not freezing. Walking through the grove in fall becomes a trip through a golden palace. Sunlight intensifies the feeling that the air itself is colored. It is like walking through gauzy gilt curtains. The glory lasts only a short time. The leaves fall, and turn brown, rotting among the dying grasses and other forbs.

I seldom go into my aspen groves in winter, for the snow there lies in deep drifts, ensuring enough moisture for next year's growth. The little creek and springs in the center of the grove freeze and disappear under the snow.

There is always something going on in the aspens. This spring I watched a woodpecker chiseling into the bark for grubs. Sometimes a covey of grouse or partridges startle out. For many years, a doe and generations after her have raised their fawns up there. Great Horned Owls used to have a nest in one of the rare, large trees. It finally toppled, and the owls are gone. Flickers, chickadees, warblers, juncos, and others call aspen groves home during the spring and summer.

It is a busy place for those five months, sung to by the trembling leaves.

SHAMUS

There never before was a dog like this, and there shall never again be another.

For he was a mutt, a mongrel, captured off the streets in Livingston for being a "man about town." I discovered him at the Stafford Animal Shelter where he'd been incarcerated for three and a half months. I wanted an Australian Shepherd, but all they had were labs, German shepherds, and pit bulls, most of them crosses. They were all dark-colored and eager to talk to me, but one dog, white with black and brown markings sat back in the corner of his kennel. I asked about him and took him out for a walk. He did well, sitting on command and behaving on the leash. The next day I took him home, his forever home. The shelter advertised him as three years old, but I believe nine months would have been more accurate, as he still didn't lift his leg to urinate, he chewed a lot on bushes in the yard, and he grew for the next three months.

His head looked as though it had St. Bernard ancestry, but without the big floppy lips. He had one black ear and one brown, both covered in soft puppy-like fur. The hair of the black patches on his body grew longer and coarser than the white hair. A perfect black heart covered his right flank. His legs were brown speckled, his body black speckled. The shelter listed him as part hound. I wondered if perhaps he came from an English setter ancestor because of the feathering on his legs and tail. I asked my vet what she thought about his lineage. She said, "Oh, I'd say about 14 different breeds."

I soon discovered that all he wanted was out. He had been too long a free spirit in town, and in a short time started clearing the four-foot chain-link fence confining him. Going after him or calling did no good. Eventually he would return and allow himself to be captive once more.

We added a radio wire to the fence, the kind that delivers a shock through the dog's special collar at three feet away. This he respected, unless something exciting came up outside the yard, such as coyotes or a car arriving. Shamus would approach the fence slowly then run and sail over it. You could almost see him gritting his teeth preparing for the shock.

He learned tricks quickly: the standards of sit up, shake hands, catch treats, and roll over. When I sat on the floor, he'd come to me, duck his head between his forelegs, and with some help, somersault. This trick he invented.

I had taught my first dachshund, Dunkel, to ring a bell by the door to be let out. I had no success teaching the Corgis or Great Pyrenees to do this. Shamus, however, picked it up on his own. He would use his foot to violently whap the three-foot piece of sleigh bells hung by the door. Of course, I'd come running to let him out.

He loved going to my cabin in northwest Montana, riding up there in the back of the pickup (with a shell on it). He barked at all bicycles, motorcycles, and trucks, but fortunately, not at cars, as he had a thunderous voice.

The first trip up there in winter, he ran out to the middle of the frozen lake. I had no idea about the thickness of the ice. My mind raced, thinking of ways to rescue him if he fell through the ice. Flipping the inverted boat over and going after him, pushing along with an oar seemed the only viable one. Blessedly, the ice held his weight, and he soon returned to my frantic cries.

One summer, a river otter visited the lake for a time. He and Shamus played together. Otter would swim near the dock where he lifted out of the water so his front legs were showing. I could almost hear him saying, "Dog, come play with me." Shamus would jump in, swim to where he'd seen him, paddle about in circles, looking down into the water, and finally return to the dock. Soon the otter returned, teasing again.

One day, when out in the boat with my three dogs, Otter popped up about five feet from us. Shamus immediately put his front paws on the side of the boat and kicked off. Fortunately, we did not capsize. They again played hide and seek until Otter grew weary of the game. Shamus climbed onto shore, and Otter left us.

In the winter, he would play King of the Hill on the five-foot pile of snow I shoveled off the patio. He always jumped to the top first to be king. When the other dogs tried to dethrone him in brief shoving and growling matches, he easily pushed them off his snow hill.

Shamus weighed 84 pounds in his prime. I used him to pull a sled with a hay bale on it to feed the sheep. He would go up the hill, following a path of his own choosing while I tried to keep up and toss pads of feed out behind the sled. I also had him drag hay bales up from the stack to the barn.

The pasture above the house is enclosed in sheep fencing with two rows of barbed wire atop it. Shamus kept escaping this to run away. I walked the fence several times looking for places he could get out, but found none. One day when we had fresh snow and he had run off, I checked the road. There were his tracks, coming out of the creek bottom on the upper side of the road. I followed them and found they came out of the 50-foot-long-culvert. Somehow, he discovered he could go on the lower side of the creek, crawl through the culvert, and be free again. Unfortunately, one winter, ice had built up in the upper end and blocked the exit. He couldn't turn around, and he didn't come to my frantic calls at the lower end of the culvert. I ran back to the house and got a tamping bar, pickax, and shovel from the barn, threw them in the car, and returned. When I started pounding on the thick ice, Shamus backed down out of his prison. He never went into it again.

He and Sable, the Australian Shepherd I bought to be his playmate, loved to run off together. Twice they encountered skunks. I arrived just in time to see them waltzing around the first skunk. Shamus dove in after it and was hit full in the face and mouth with the spray. He choked, vomited, and started rubbing his head in the dirt. He kept hacking and pawing at his face as I walked him home. I rinsed his mouth out with the hose and washed his face as best I could. Then I mixed up the recommended hydrogen peroxide, soap, baking soda, and water solution to wash him off. Sable had somehow avoided the spray and killed the skunk.

The second time they met up with Mephitis mephitis, Shamus stayed back and left Sable on her own. That skunk survived, and Sable was only lightly sprayed.

As he grew older, he refused to get in the rowboat at the lake but would follow us along the shore. The next year that became too much, and he would stay on the dock or go back to the cabin. He could no longer jump in the back of the pickup but could get in the second seat of the cab with a little help. At 14, he had surgery to remove a tumor on his pancreas. This gave him another year and a half of basically good life, but his hindquarters weakened until I had to send him over the Rainbow Bridge.

Shamus was the consummate watchdog: my guardian, my protector, and my defender. I shall forever see his black and white plume of tail racing ahead of me up the hill in the deep grass or through the snow—the free spirit and wonder dog.

YEAR OF THE RODENTS

In the order of mammals, rodents have the highest number of species. This year there was an explosion of all the common rodents we have here. My neighbors and I, here in the country, all complained to each other about the profusion of voles (meadow mice). As the snows melted in March and April, a maze of the voles' winter tunneling work came to light.

Over half our snow fell in November and December. The final tally of 115 inches was the fourth lowest in 38 years. Perhaps the open winter with more available feed let them multiply as only rodents can. Their little winding half tunnels in the topsoil and dead plants are everywhere.

We also had more pocket gopher diggings than usual. These dirt casts are pushed up under the snow during the winter and look like heavy ropes or cables lying on the surface of the soil.

I am currently feeding seven chipmunks. They are better to watch than a nature film—squabbling, running straight up the cement retaining wall, stuffing cheek pockets full of seeds, and dashing off with about two teaspoons of winter food. A friend suggested I follow them to their nest and check out their caches. They can outrun me at least ten to one, racing across the top of the chain-link fence, then from pole to pole of the driveway rail fence and disappearing into the wilderness of the chokecherry bushes along the creek. They personify greased lightning.

I also feed at least two squirrels. In June, momma squirrel came to the feeders on the patio retaining wall with two youngsters trailing her. They quickly grew to adult size, and only one squirrel now comes up from the barn. Another lives in the apple trees south of the house. They have learned to get peanuts out of the feeder I made for them on the deck. They also make the death-defying run under the deck, across the patio, and up the retaining wall. If both converge at the same time, they engage in battle until one runs off, generally chased by the victor. I have also seen a squirrel run off the rabbit that comes into the garden behind the retaining wall. Rabbits aren't rodents, but also seemed to have a good reproductive year. There were four in the yard at one time in November. They have a trail in the snow from the creek to the house where there is a dish of cracked corn for them in cold weather

Unfortunately, rats were also prolific this year. Karen, my neighbor a third of a mile up the road, had a pack rat in her car that ate the windshield wiper tubes and much of the covering off the wiring in the engine. My neighbors, Barb and Mike, one half mile to the west, had one chew up all the wiring in their hot tub, plus tunneling into the insulation. The hot tub was a total loss. Pack rats also moved into my barn, creating two huge nests of dead leaves and sticks. Their odor is their most offensive quality. It is an intense urine and feces smell, not to be forgotten. I live-trapped one in the barn and gave him a car ride two miles west to the top of the Bozeman Pass where there was tall grass by a small forest. Prior to this, the dogs discovered a rat under the lawnmower stored under the deck. They chased it down and killed it when I moved the mower for them. Oddly enough it was a Norway rat, the common "city rat." The pack rats, or bushy-tailed wood rats have rather pretty faces, much like chinchillas. Norways don't.

I've also had to set up a trap line for mice in the basement, laundry room, and car. I trapped a dozen or more this fall. A flat tire this winter forced me to get out the spare. The bolt that held it down was extremely difficult to remove. When I lifted out the tire I discovered why. The area beneath it was packed full of stuffing from my car seats, and beneath all that was about a gallon of sunflower and other seeds. Three mummified mice were included in the nesting. Cleanup was long and odorous.

Mice demonstrated the rodent power of gnawing and chewed into the ceiling and wood panel walls of the interior of the chicken coop, which has been abandoned for a dozen years. The threat of Hanta Virus disease has kept me from tearing out the interior walls and ceiling to clear the mess of mice and insulation.

I had help on this project in August when a bear visited and tore siding off the front and back of the coop. I can only surmise that he was after the mice in the walls. His claw marks and muddy paw prints remain on the building. The insulation had been reduced to sort of granular debris. Cleanup was tedious, but gave me a great deal of kindling and a large garbage sack of what used to be insulation. I'm not as angry at the bear as at the mice and possibly rats for this destruction. I do hope that the bear had a good meal of rodent for all the work it did pulling off shiplap siding.

Basically, the rodents are the second link in life's food chain. Many birds and mammals dine on them as their major food source. Owls, hawks, magpies, foxes, coyotes, weasels, and others have them as a main food source or for snacks. Twice I saw the chickens kill mice. One almost strangled to death trying to eat a mouse whole. I managed to pull the mouse out in time and give the chicken mouth to beak resuscitation. It lived.

This was a year the rodents won. Voles or pocket gophers killed the young silver poplar tree I've been nurturing the past four years. Some rodent decimated the patch of my violas in the flower garden, ate a young hollyhock and columbines down to the ground, and plowed up one neighbor's lawn.

I should be more forgiving of creatures whose primary reason for being is to be a food source. They are expensive, however, and irritating. Mother Nature knows what she's doing, though. I suppose the entertainment of squirrels and chipmunks outweighs the destruction of the others. Living in the country has pluses and minuses.

Hoarfrost

SOLID WATER

Frost is beautiful. Hoarfrost collects on grass, twigs, barbed wire, and old flower stalks, anything in the out-of-doors, layering onto crystals up to two inches long. A breeze makes them fall like snow onto the surfaces beneath. Frost on windows is even lovelier, forming feathery whorls, snowflake-like crystals, spots, and ornate baroque pictures. But the freezing fog that causes this passes quickly and the enchanted landscape loses its white coating, returning to drab tans, yellows, and grays.

This January I drove to Helena. For over 70 miles, the landscape had been transformed into a crystal-coated conduit. Heavy hoarfrost coated all the plants. I felt as though I drove through a Disney-generated landscape. Every leafless dogwood, willow, and cottonwood was bedecked in greater beauty than their leaves give them. The roadside forbs and grasses were clothed, as the Bible says, "richer than Solomon in all his glory." On the return trip, four hours later, silver and white raiment had vanished, and only naked bark, dead grasses, and weeds remained.

Usually snow lasts much longer. Too long in a bitter winter or late spring. At first a few flakes float down, landing on my dark sleeve, so I can see the fragile, six-armed crystals. Then more fall, infinite in variety. And more, until the lawn and pastures are white. These delicate pieces of frozen water pile up; an inch, six inches, a foot, two feet, and in the unfortunate recipients of lake-effect snow back east—six feet. All from tiny flakes one can barely see.

If the wind should come, it makes drifts—drifts hard enough to walk on, hard enough to stop a car, hard enough to high-center a pickup. All from lovely crystals fragile as gossamer glass.

There is beauty in snowdrifts, too. Lines and crescents catch behind blades of grass, snow fences, sagebrush, and any barrier that slows the wind enough to make it drop its load. Long waves of drifts may form, frozen sculptures that a change of wind direction can rearrange. Cornices develop off a mountain ridge or a roof, and extend into impossibly long hanging rolls.

I read that rain starts as ice crystals in high clouds. As these fall through warmer air, the crystals melt.

Sometimes up-drafts in thunderheads lift the rain back up again and again freezing, coating, and enlarging the ice drop into hail. I have seen it hail enough that snowplows had to be brought out to clear the highways. Hail can break windows, dent cars, and ruin roofs and wood siding.

I prefer the delicate dendrites of frost that can make a window a transient work of art, the plates of hoarfrost, and the amazing tiny crystals we call snow. Solid water is an artistic magician's plaything.

LORI MICKEN

REMNANTS

In 24 years, we wore out four sets of sheets.
They became rags, and now are gone.
In 24 years, towels became too worn,
And now are for the dogs, or gone.
In 24 years, shy only a week of 25,
You packed all your things, and are gone.

The garden has gone to grass,
The cattle and sheep are gone
To market, or friends' flocks.
The corrals have broken poles,
And rotted, leaning posts.
The barn is stable, only a window gone.

The land and I are all that's left,
And I am on the way to gone.

DRAGONFLY SERMON

I sit on the dock at the cabin, one of my three favorite places on earth. Dragonflies, killers of other insects, abound here. Most are black with heavy abdomens and smoky-blue decorations along their head and back.

I discover a dragonfly naiad crawling painfully up a sedge stalk. It is an ugly creature, the color of lake bottom, with blotches of darker brown, and body slightly flattened, top to bottom. It pauses, pulses, seems to be gasping its last. For an hour, I read and watch the lake turn from a mirror to riffles and back.

Legs locked on the narrow stalk, an aquatic creature committing suicide, leaving its home for a foreign planet, headed into the unknown with only the intent of instinct.

Fish jump, leaving spreading circles on the lake. A mallard takes off, quacking, and circles the lake. Bubbles of gas from decomposition rise like silver balls and leave more circles.

I keep reading and observing my insect. Another hour is gone. The exoskeleton has split on the back, and along with the gills, is desiccated. A gray-blue thorax arches out of the widening split. The head and curved ebony body of a Phoenix arches up and free of the sarcophagus that was itself. Little nubbins appear on the thorax. The knobs spread and stretch, slowly becoming four transparent wings, each an inch and a half long, etched with veins unique to its species. There should be a shout of victory or a cry of rebirth, but all is silence.

The creature still clings to the dried shell of its abandoned body. Its abdomen pulses, breathing pure air, rather than filtering it from the water. Eyes with a hundred facets, bulging like turrets from the broad head, reflect light in rainbow beauty. It dries above its former liquid home and suddenly, flies! Its instincts, too, were processing, pulsing, swelling, until something changed, and it knew to become a creature of the air.

I sit, paralyzed with wonder, and watch other dragonflies skim the water and rise to the sky.

Maybe in the future, I, too, will crawl somewhere, split my back, spread wings, and take flight into some strange new medium unimaginable by a human. No resurrection could be more wondrous than what I've observed here at water's edge.

Be sure to read the companion to this book,
Ninety Years in Montana—

***Eighty Years
in Montana***

by Lori Micken

Also available on Amazon.com

ASPEN SPRINGS PUBLISHING

40 SUNFLOWER LANE
LIVINGSTON, MT 59047

Made in the USA
Middletown, DE
30 November 2023

44162078R00102